D1106858

TRUMBULL STICKNEY

TRUMBULL STICKNEY

Amberys R. Whittle

Lewisburg
Bucknell University Press

© 1973 by Associated University Presses, Inc.

Associated University Presses, Inc.
Cranbury, New Jersey 08512

Library of Congress Cataloging in Publication Data
Whittle, Amberys R
 Trumbull Stickney.

 Bibliography: p.
 1. Stickney, Trumbull, 1874–1904.
PS3537.T525Z95   811'.4   72–425
ISBN 0–8387–1154–5

Printed in the United States of America

 Chapter 1, "The Life of Trumbull Stickney," also appears as the introduction to Amberys R. Whittle, ed., *The Poems of Trumbull Stickney,* Farrar, Straus & Giroux, Inc., 1972. Reprinted by permission of Farrar, Straus & Giroux, Inc.
 Chapter 7, "The Theme of Time," appeared in a briefer form in *The Sewanee Review* 74 (Autumn 1966) : 899–914. Copyright 1966 by Amberys R. Whittle.
 Some other portions of this book © Amberys R. Whittle, 1969.

To my wife, Natalie

Contents

Preface

America has ignored few of its poets of merit so completely as it has Trumbull Stickney. He lived most of his brief life (1874–1904) abroad, obtaining a *doctorat ès lettres* from the University of Paris, and thus was one of the first modern scholar-poets. His poems, last collected in 1905, have long been out of print and could be found only in a few anthologies; but they are available now, in an edition prepared by myself recently published by Farrar, Straus & Giroux, Inc.

Stickney deserves reconsideration on the part of critics of literature, many of whom have ignored or misread him, tending to type him as a representative late nineteenth-century American poet. But Stickney's verse proves baffling when he is so read. I have attempted throughout this study to correct that misconception and to guide the reader toward a better understanding of the poet.

Because detailed information concerning Stickney's life has been difficult to obtain, the first chapter is primarily biographical. A survey of poetry at the end of the century provides a context against which Stickney's achievements may be judged. A discussion of his prose has been included because it is interesting in itself and provides a further perspective on the poetry. Chapter four reveals how modern critics have evaluated Stickney as a poet. The last three chapters examine Stickney's interest in dramatic forms of verse; his use of land-scape imagery, including a unique kind; and his pervasive concern with time and its implications.

With the exception of a few early poems, Stickney's verse, as quoted in this critical study, is taken from the 1905 edition, *The Poems of Trumbull Stickney.*

A. R. W.

Des Moines, Iowa

Acknowledgments

I wish to thank the many libraries that have made their resources available to me while the present study was being prepared, especially those at Harvard University, the Boston Public Library, the Massachusetts Historical Society, Yale University, Duke University, the University of North Carolina, and the University of Chicago. I am also grateful to Drake University for a grant that allowed me some time for research and writing.

The following people have been most generous in allowing me to quote from unpublished or from published sources, and I wish to express my sincere appreciation to them:

Mr. Charles F. Adams, for permission to quote from Henry Adams, *The Life of George Cabot Lodge*, 1911.

Professor Maurice F. Brown, Jr., of Oakland University, for permission to quote from his 1958 Harvard doctoral dissertation, *Harvard Poetic Renaissance: 1885–1910*.

Mr. George C. Lodge, for permission to quote from the letters of his grandfather, George Cabot Lodge; from a letter from Henry Adams to George Cabot Lodge; and from Henry Adams, *The Life of George Cabot Lodge*, 1911.

Mr. William B. Mason and Mr. Robert A. Jansen, Trust Officer of Union Trust Company, Stamford, Connecticut, for permission to quote from Daniel Gregory Mason's *Music in My Time,* 1938.

Mr. Stephen T. Riley, Director of the Massachusetts Historical Society, for permission to quote from the Lodge papers in the collection on deposit with the Society.

Mrs. Louise Tanner, for permission to quote from Trumbull Stickney's letters.

Mr. Edmund Wilson, for permission to quote from "The Country I Remember," *The New Republic* 103 (October 14, 1940). (Copyright © 1940, 1968, 1972 by Edmund Wilson.)

I also wish to thank the following publishers for giving me permission to quote from published works:

Farrar, Straus & Giroux, Inc., for permission to reprint the Introduction to *The Poems of Trumbull Stickney,* ed. Amberys R. Whittle, 1972. (Copyright © 1966, 1969, 1972 by Amberys R. Whittle from *The Poems of Trumbull Stickney.* Reprinted by arrangement with Farrar, Straus & Giroux, Inc.)

Holt, Rinehart and Winston, Inc., for permission to quote from Norman Hapgood, *The Changing Years,* 1930.

The Macmillan Company, for permission to quote from Madison Cawein, *Poems,* 1911. (Copyright, 1911, by The Macmillan Company.) Also for permission to quote from *Literary History of the United States: History,* 3rd ed., revised, ed. Robert E. Spiller *et al.,* 1963. (Copyright © 1946, 1947, 1948, 1953, 1963 by the Macmillan Company.)

The University of the South, for permission to reprint, in an expanded form, my article "The Dust of Seasons: Time in the Poetry of Trumbull Stickney," *The Sewanee Review* 74 (Autumn 1966): 899–914. (Copyright © 1966 by Amberys R. Whittle.)

TRUMBULL STICKNEY

1

The Life of Trumbull Stickney[1]

According to the testimony of gifted and esteemed men, Joseph Trumbull Stickney was one of the best-educated, most highly cultivated and talented Americans during his brief life (1874–1904). The majority of this life was spent abroad; this plus his pursuit of one of the most demanding of academic degrees of the time, the *doctorat ès lettres* of the University of Paris, has helped to make him an obscure figure, even for those who know that two volumes of verse bear his name. One who studies the record carefully will not think it an exaggeration to state that Trumbull Stickney was a singular individual, one of those rare products only occasionally produced by a culture.

Stickney was descended from prominent New England families.[2] Austin Stickney, his father, was a classical scholar;

1. Copyright © 1966, 1969, 1972 by Amberys R. Whittle from *The Poems of Trumbull Stickney*. Reprinted by arrangement with Farrar, Straus & Giroux, Inc.

2. For many details relating to the life of Trumbull Stickney I am indebted to a dissertation written at Princeton University in 1949 by Thomas Riggs, Jr., *Trumbull Stickney (1874–1904)*. This dissertation was made available through University Microfilms, Inc., in 1955 (Publication No. 11,006).

he was educated in the Boston area and entered Harvard in 1848. After teaching for several years he returned to Harvard, obtaining his M.A. in 1858, when he went to Trinity College in Hartford as Professor of Latin and Greek to remain until 1864. In 1863 Professor Stickney married Harriet Champion Trumbull, whose ancestors included Jonathan Trumbull, a governor of Connecticut during the Colonial period. She was eleven years younger than Professor Stickney, strong-willed, and wealthy.

It seems that Professor Stickney was not a man of much imagination. His scholarly work consists mostly of editions of the classics, several of Cicero, done in a pedantic, impersonal manner. Perhaps such a temperament helps to account for the somewhat unusual life he was soon to lead, due, it would seem, to the determination of his wife.[3] In 1864, as Thomas Riggs, Jr., puts it, "three years before Mark Twain and the trip of the *Quaker City* inaugurated the tourist era of American relations with Europe, the Stickneys set out upon their travels: for Rome, for Paris, for Dresden, Nice, Florence, Geneva, London, Venice, New York, to merge with the restless group whose figures crowd the pages of the novels of Henry James."[4] The family remained abroad until 1879, returning only for a brief semester at Hartford in 1870. Of the four children, Trumbull Stickney was the first male and third child. He was born outside Geneva on June 20, 1874. From 1879 until 1891 the family passed back and forth between New York and Europe and began spending time in

Riggs talked to many people then living who knew Stickney, including the poet's brother, and he had access to some letters no longer available. His work, which is primarily a biography and a study of Stickney's place in the literary scene, will thus remain a basic source for anyone interested in Stickney.

3. Years later George Cabot Lodge was to write, "It has evidently been simply her desire that has waltzed them round Europe for all these years." An unpublished letter of April 14 [1896?] in the Massachusetts Historical Society. Quoted by permission of the Society and George Cabot Lodge.

4. Riggs, p. 14.

England as well, where Mrs. Stickney and her daughter Eliza, then twenty-three years old, were presented at Court in 1885.

Such a life must have been rich in experience for the children, but "both Joe and his brother Henry looked back with some bitterness upon their early wanderings as depriving them of the normal contacts of childhood and the advantages of locality,"[5] an attitude reflected in the mood of rootlessness and exile in Stickney's poetry. Although his wanderings limited his own involvement in academic affairs to browsing through libraries, editing texts, and forming friendships with people of scholarly interests such as King John of Saxony, Professor Stickney did give his son Trumbull (the name he preferred in later years) a thorough education in the classics. Professor Stickney also taught his son to play the violin. In the fall of 1890 the Sticneys were back in New York, where Trumbull attended Dr. Cutler's school to prepare for Harvard; only once before and for a brief period had Trumbull Stickney attended a school.

Stickney entered Harvard at the age of seventeen in the fall of 1891. William Vaughn Moody describes his appearance and the impression he made at that time: "He was then, and he remained until the end of his life, a picture of radiant youth—very tall, a figure supple and graceful as a Greek runner's, a face of singular brightness moulded upon lines of earnest strength, a demeanor in which boyish simplicity was combined with implications of an experience more rich and a social habit more complex than our New World civilization affords."[6] At this period the elective system was in operation at Harvard, and the grip of the classics upon the students had been weakened considerably. Nevertheless, Trumbull

---

5. *Ibid.*, p. 24.
6. William Vaughn Moody, "The Poems of Trumbull Stickney," *The North American Review* 183 (November 16, 1906) : 1006.

Stickney took the old required courses. In addition to the classics, he was to study under Josiah Royce in philosophy and under Charles Rockwell Lanman, who later taught T. S. Eliot, in Sanskrit. His instructor in Latin and Greek was Morris Hickey Morgan, who became his friend and was instrumental in bringing him back to Harvard as an instructor after his later studies in Paris. Near the beginning of his first semester Stickney wrote his sister Lucy, eight years older than he but to whom he seems to have been closest among the members of the family, "my greatest joy is Greek tragedy in which I foresee I shall be lost for the next 2000 years."[7]

There was, however, a difference between Trumbull Stickney and the other students: the New World does not always accept the old or those who have been shaped by it. George Santayana, who was also teaching at Harvard, describes an instance of such rejection. A group of students led by Julian Codman met in his room in the evening for what Julian called "poetry bees."[8] The group did not accept Stickney, as Santayana explains:

> I had a friend who was himself a poet, exceptionally cultivated, and educated by his father (an unemployed teacher) to perfection: Joe, or, as he preferred to call himself, Trumbull Stickney. I once tried to introduce him into our readings; but no, it wouldn't do. Julian confidentially informed me that "the others didn't like him." Why not? Because he had mentioned the sunset and called it "gorgeous." I understood that he was too literary and ladylike for Harvard: and I myself found him more companionable later in Paris, where my memory prefers to place him.[9]

If "poetry bees" were closed to Stickney, and one is re-

---

7. Quoted by permission of Mrs. Louise Tanner.
8. George Santayana, *The Middle Span*, vol. 2 of *Persons and Places* (New York: Charles Scribner's Sons, 1945), p. 102.
9. *Ibid.*, p. 103.

minded of Milton at Cambridge, other activities were to benefit from his accomplishments. The only freshman in the *Conférence Française*'s production of *Le Bourgeois Gentilhomme* was Trumbull Stickney, who played the lead. In the audience sat Edwin Arlington Robinson, at Harvard that year as a special student. The Harvard of these years has been characterized by some as inferior to the older tradition, probably because less emphasis was given to the classics; but Norman Hapgood, who was there several years before Stickney, characterizes it as having a healthy atmosphere of questioning.[10] Robinson and Stickney are only two of many in whom this prevailing tone is reflected, although it often goes beyond Hapgood's description to something darker and more pessimistic.

Trumbull Stickney was also the first freshman ever to be elected to the Board of Editors of *The Harvard Monthly*. Robert Morss Lovett, the Editor-in-Chief, describes his first impressions of Stickney:

> In college dramatics he took with equal ease parts in Latin, French, or German. At our first meeting, as he stood in his doorway to admit me, I saw a tall, very handsome youth with a charming dignity touched by a shade of deference. He read me several poems, and I engaged him at once for the *Monthly*.[11]

Stickney seems to have been the kind of person who has not a great many friends but a few remarkable ones entirely devoted to him; such was to be the case with Lovett:

> I was a graduate student and assistant in English. Stickney was a sophomore, but during this year when Moody was in Europe [1892–93] I found in the former my chief companionship. Officially I read his themes; unofficially, his poetry. An attack

10. Norman Hapgood, *The Changing Years* (New York: Farrar & Rinehart, Inc., 1930), pp. 74 ff.
11. Robert Morss Lovett, *All Our Years* (New York: The Viking Press, 1948), p. 41.

of measles confined him to his room, where I tended him, without a thought of spreading the disease.[12]

The Harvard Monthly of these years was one of the best college publications in the country.[13] To it Stickney was to contribute as an undergraduate over two dozen poems, as well as a good amount of prose including book reviews, literary essays, and short stories; and he continued to appear in it while in Paris. In 1892 he also contributed two poems to *The Mahogany Tree*, a short-lived magazine edited by another Harvard poet, Philip Henry Savage, about whom he wrote in a letter to his sister Lucy, "Savage calls me James Thomson Stickney,"[14] although the poems Savage printed do not indicate such an influence. Stickney's success with the *Monthly* was in sharp contrast to the experience of Edwin Arlington Robinson. As Emery Neff observes,

> None of Robinson's poems was accepted by the *Monthly*, whose poetry columns he was not far wrong in thinking a monopoly of its editors. During that academic year 1891–92, three-quarters of its verse was written by Moody, Hugh McCulloch, Philip Savage, Trumbull Stickney, and Samuel Duffield of the editorial staff, Moody appearing in almost every number.[15]

William Vaughn Moody finished his college program in three years and was abroad in 1892–93, after which time he returned for graduate work. He and Stickney must have met through the *Monthly* during the latter's freshman year. The two had much in common: both were young poets with a knowledge of the classics preparing for careers as teachers;

---

12. *Ibid.*
13. This magazine and the group of writers for whom it was an important outlet will be treated in more detail in chapter 2.
14. Quoted in Riggs, p. 48, and used here by permission of Mrs. Louise Tanner. The original letter has disappeared.
15. Emery Neff, *Edwin Arlington Robinson* (New York: William Sloane Associates, Inc., 1948), p. 26.

both were to die young of the same disease.[16] This friendship
was to develop and continue during the Paris years.

Another friend—he was to become his closest—was George
Cabot Lodge, known familiarly as "Bay," the son of Senator
Henry Cabot Lodge. Evidently he and Stickney met in their
senior year; even though they were of different tempera-
ments, there was much to unite them. Bay Lodge was bright,
energetic, with a tendency toward the self-dramatic, and with
a strong ambition to be a poet, if he could only manage to
walk the tightrope between rebelliousness and family responsibility.[17] Lodge visited the Sticwith a strong; and, although he
found Professor Stickney intelligent, he complained in several
letters to his mother of his lack of cheerfulness:

> I have taken a good many meals there lately & I tell you it
> requires all my robustness to preserve me from utter gloom.
> There is an atmosphere of inanition & utter unenthusiasm &
> lifelessness about the whole family that causes me to wonder
> that Joe has come out as well as he has. I don't believe "I was
> ever a fighter" [his own motto] was ever remotely thought of
> by any of them except Joe. They are quite forlorn. . . . It is
> indescribable & I don't see how Joe bears it.[18]

The portrait is interesting because it shows the general sense
of restraint which evidently became a part of Stickney's intellectual make-up, often becoming pessimism, and which
seems to have warred at times with his natural enthusiasm
and openness. Lodge himself was later succinctly described

16. For a rather extended list of striking similarities between these two
poets, see David D. Henry, *William Vaughn Moody, A Study* (Boston: Bruce
Humphries, Inc., 1934), p. 156.
17. In addition to the many details to be found in Riggs, there is *The
Life of George Cabot Lodge* by Henry Adams (Boston and New York:
Houghton Mifflin Company, 1911), as well as unpublished letters in the
Massachusetts Historical Society.
18. A letter in the collection of the Massachusetts Historical Society. The
date November 14, 1894, has been added. Riggs dates it a year later, which
does seem reasonable, on p. 292. By permission of the Society and George
Cabot Lodge.

in a letter from Henry James to Henry Adams: "I recall him as so intelligent and open and delightful,—a great and abundant social luxury."[19] Edith Wharton was very fond of the young man.

Stickney and Lodge decided to continue their studies in Paris after their graduation from Harvard in 1895. The Stickney family lived at 55 Avenue Marceau and Lodge around the corner. The two young men began their studies at the University of Paris in the fall of 1895. Lodge found the program quite demanding:

> The exactitude & the accuracy & profundity of the scholarship is unknown in Cambridge. When I came here I thought I knew a little something about literature. I really from their standards know almost nothing. For instance a man here spends 4 years on Dante. . . . The specializing is tremendous. The idea of taking a century of literature in one year as they do in Cambridge would seem preposterous.[20]

Stickney seems to have settled down to the demands of his studies without much trouble, although he thought some of the historical scholarship dull. Some of his letters suggest that he might have wished more freedom from family control.

Family demands were to be of concern to Lodge during his year's study in Paris. His father, who had studied history under Henry Adams and taught at Harvard, had been elected to the Senate in 1892. In a dispute between Britain and Venezuela over the British Guiana-Venezuela boundary, Senator Lodge supported and was a chief advocate of the United States settling the argument in a way that would prevent any British expansion. While his father was making

---

19. Quoted by Adams in a letter to Elizabeth Cameron, September 4, 1909. See *Letters of Henry Adams* (1892–1918), ed. Worthington Chauncey Ford (Boston and New York: Houghton Mifflin Company, 1938), p. 522 n.

20. A letter to his mother dated December 1895, in the collection of the Massachusetts Historical Society. By permission of the Society and George Cabot Lodge.

speeches on the floor of the senate, Lodge questioned the value of his life as a student and as a poet dependent upon his father.[21] The crisis eventually passed. The next fall Lodge was at the University of Berlin, where he read Schopenhauer. His first volume of verse was published in 1898, a year which also provided a chance for action with the outbreak of the Spanish-American War; Lodge joined the navy at once and saw active service.

Lodge describes Stickney's state of mind in several letters home during the period 1895–96. One of these is especially interesting:

> He has settled into a mute, not uncheerful despair, says he has given up all his "morning wishes" [the latter word is not clear] poetry etc & is a man dead & dry as far as art is concerned. He says he knows he can make a good scholar . . . & that he might as well give up poetry first & last—he has got to earn his bread.[22]

Lodge's letters home had been somewhat critical of the Stickneys' lack of concern with American foreign policy, but he was alarmed when Theodore Roosevelt wrote him saying, "Don't let the worthless society of Emigré-Americans in Paris & London influence you to harm - - - - - - I do not think they could persuade you that life was not strife etc." After relating the incident to his mother, who evidently later denied that Roosevelt meant the Stickneys, Lodge continued:

> When I remember what I have written to you & Pa & that he has been staying in Washington I know he must mean the Stickneys & by the last phrase Joe. I am very sorry because the Stickneys have been tremendously kind to me & though I don't approve of the way they live or their point of view I

---

21. Several of the letters in the collection of the Massachusetts Historical Society deal with this struggle in the mind of George Cabot Lodge; he was annoyed that the Stickneys seemed indifferent to American foreign policy.

22. A letter to which the date December 1895 has been added, in the collection of the Massachusetts Historical Society. By permission of the Society and George Cabot Lodge.

don't mean anyone to know it but you & Pa. As for Joe he is about the best friend I have. . . . I think he has been unfortunately brought up & is having a hard time in consequence, but I believe he will pull through & I am sure he has great talents.

Lodge went on to admit that there were times when for him too there seemed to be "nothing but dry grey air," a phrase he attributed to Stickney.[23]

Lodge and Stickney are not the only scholar-poets of modern times to feel oppressed when the demands on their time and attention become too great to allow for much creativity. There were, however, other sides to the experiences of this year. Stickney and Henry Adams walked the streets of Paris discussing Greek philosophy. He and Lodge had formed in the winter of 1895–96[24] an organization to which the much older Adams was drawn: "Bay Lodge and Joe Stickney had given birth to the wholly new and original party of Conservative Christian Anarchists, to restore true poetry under the inspiration of the 'Götterdämmerung.' "[25] The whole thing was, as an Adams scholar has called it, "a gossamer invention,"[26] but it allowed for a good deal of wit involving the Hegelian thesis, antithesis, and synthesis, along with a mixture of irony and pessimism. The relationship among these three men has been aptly described by Elizabeth Stevenson:

Stickney and Lodge found in Henry Adams their own ardors and despairs pushed beyond their focus into something frightening but interesting. And he was good to them; a good listener,

23. A letter to which the date March 1896 with a question mark has been added, in the collection of the Massachusetts Historical Society. By permission of the Society and George Cabot Lodge.

24. This date is "arrived at deductively" and explained in Riggs, p. 294, n. 2.

25. *The Education of Henry Adams* (Boston and New York: Houghton Mifflin Company, 1927) , p. 405.

26. Harold Dean Cater, ed., *Henry Adams and His Friends* (Boston: Houghton Mifflin Company, 1947) , p. lxxxii. This book contains inaccurate information on Stickney's birth and schooling.

a good reader of their verses. On his side, Adams liked the two young men for the freshness of their notions. Even their disillusionment was dazzlingly young. He hoped for much for them and quenched some of his unhappiness in their tonic desires.[27]

In his biography of Lodge, who outlived Stickney by only a few years, Adams remarked that "Stickney owned a nature of singular refinement, and his literary work promised to take rank at the head of the work done by his generation of Americans."[28]

In his studies Stickney had reached the point where he could be more objective about the Greek culture to which he had been drawn. He sadly began to discern the "limits of great minds."[29] His awareness of the dark side of Greek life was to deepen. In a review of Burckhardt he wrote,

Le mensonge est grec par excellence; la vengeance, un dogme, et la méchanceté, telle qu'elle paraît à la tribune et dans le monde, d'un raffinement étonnant. Que l'on n'aille pas parler des philosophes. Sans doute, l'idéal a son prix; mais, pour bien juger, on doit regarder à la pratique et, en Grèce, il y a loin de l'un à l'autre. Du reste, on n'a qu'à y entendre parler de la vie.[30]

All this reflects indirectly his growing admiration for the literature and civilization of ancient India. Sylvain Lévi, a pioneer in French studies in Sanskrit and India, was his teacher and adviser. He, like Stickney, was also a Hellenist and made comparative studies. Before Stickney left Paris he and Lévi translated the Bhagavad-Gita together.[31]

27. Elizabeth Stevenson, *Henry Adams* (New York: The Macmillan Company, 1955) , p. 298.
28. Henry Adams, *The Life of George Cabot Lodge*, p. 119.
29. In a letter to Robert Morss Lovett. Quoted by permission of Mrs. Louise Tanner.
30. "Burckhardt (Jacob) .—Griechische Kulturgeschichte," *L'Année Sociologique* 3 (1898–1899) : 313.
31. *Bhagavad-Gītā*, traduit du sanskrit par Sylvain Lévi et J.--T. Stickney (Paris, 1938) . Madame Lévi was responsible for the publication of this book after her husband's death; it was reprinted in 1964 by A. Maisonneuve, Paris.

Stickney's father died on November 30, 1896, and was buried at Fontainbleau. In the fall of 1897, when his mother and sister went to Florence, Trumbull Stickney took the first of three lodgings in Paris away from his family. The last of these was at Rue d'Assas, near the Luxembourg gardens, where he was visited by Harvard friends, including Moody, who came in October of 1897. The added measure of freedom seems to have been invigorating. One of his visitors was his friend Robert Morss Lovett:

> My memories of the city are brightest through him. The background suited him perfectly; whether it was in his little apartment in the rue d'Assas, or, as I like to remember him, striding like a young god across the Champs Elysées to join us at Laurent's. His enthusiasm was magnificent and charmed older men, like Henry Adams.[32]

Another visitor was Santayana, who later called him one of "the three best-educated persons I have known."[33] It was here that Santayana thought he discerned a change in his young friend:

> I remember him with more pleasure in Paris during that long interval when he bloomed freely under all sorts of influences stimulating to the spirit. In his nice lodgings overlooking the quiet side of the Luxembourg gardens, or in long walks along the Seine, he would reveal his gradual change of allegiance from classic antiquity to something more troubled and warmer, more charitable, closer to the groping mind of our day, to the common people, and to the problem of America.[34]

One of Stickney's French friends was Henri Hubert, in 1897 one of the editors of the religious anthropology sections

---

32. Lovett, p. 80.
33. George Santayana, *My Host the World,* vol. 3 of *Persons and Places* (New York: Charles Scribner's Sons, 1953) , p. 28. In a letter to Thomas Riggs, Jr., from Rome, February 22, 1947, Santayana said that Stickney's mind and heart were "the most delicate that I ever knew in America." Quoted in Riggs, p. 168.
34. *Ibid., The Middle Span,* pp. 148–49.

of Émile Durkheim's *L'Année Sociologique*. An indication of the spirit of the period is the fact that Durkheim had studied suicide as a phenomenon of the times. A few years later, at the Paris Exposition of 1900, Henry Adams pondered the spiritual significance of dynamos, while Stickney grew enthusiastic over Rodin and Japanese lacquers. But underneath his aestheticism Stickney was not indifferent to the current of ideas, as his writings reveal. One suspects that he was merely trying to hold in check that tendency toward despair which Moody later described:

> Throughout his life, in spite of its fortunate outward circumstances and real happiness, there weighed upon him a nameless oppression, a sense of the futility of the worldly outcome, a shadow of pain and bitterness upon all the fair face of things. But his manner of confronting this tragedy which he saw implicit in the texture of life changed its quality both for himself and for those who knew him. The important thing was seen to be, not the nature of our destiny, but the manner in which it is met. . . . His was essentially the stoic view, but a stoicism heroic and infinitely tender, pregnant with the sweetness and strength of life.[35]

By 1900 Stickney had already written a dramatic scene on the Promethean theme, *Prometheus Pyrphoros*. In July of 1902 Moody visited him for a month, the two of them reading or rereading the entire Greek tragedy together. One result for Moody was to be *The Fire-Bringer* (1904). Lodge, who had married, made trips to Paris with his beautiful wife until 1901, after which date he and Stickney did not meet again for two years. The common experience is reflected in his *Cain* (1904) and *Herakles* (1908). Another close friend of this period was Elizabeth Cameron, friend of Henry Adams.

In 1902 Stickney published his first volume of poetry, *Dra-*

---

35. Moody, p. 1018.

matic Verses.[36] His ever-widening interests are indicated by his visit to the museum of St. Germain, where he observed a new collection of carved bones and ivory of a "prehistoric generation." For Stickney the occasion becomes an opportunity to consider the nature of change:

> As I was leaving, some one remarked that this was no longer a palace, but the people's palace. A note of Socialism in such, surroundings rang out strangely. It is characteristic, however. Old manors, old castles, old buildings of every sort all over France are being turned more and more into museums. . . . Does the old palace thereby become the people's palace? Is science really humane and social, and is the scholar so much more modest and affable than the courtier or the aristocrat? . . . The Museum of St. Germain is a great school for historic modesty. Nowhere else do you see so clearly what an orderly pandemonium it has been down here ever since the sun first rose.[37]

Or he revealed his interest in ceramics by visiting Beauvais in the country to see the oven of Delaherche, a local artist who had achieved a considerable reputation but who still lived modestly because he destroyed his imperfect creations. For Stickney, Delaherche becomes a type of the dedicated artist, "carrying out, just as well as he is able, that something human which now becomes a picture, now a statue, and, in his case, a vase, a bowl, a pitcher; shaping and coloring them as he sees them, and spending his life upon so doing; finding pleasure and duty, and using his whole love in these things— like every one who ever has done anything well worth doing and well done."[38]

Shane Leslie arrived in Paris at the age of seventeen in October of 1902 and lived near Stickney, who took him under

---

36. Trumbull Stickney, *Dramatic Verses* (Boston: Charles E. Goodspeed, 1902) .

37. *Ibid.,* "The Museum of St. Germain," *The Nation* 75 (November 20, 1902) : 398.

38. *Ibid.,* "The Beauvais Pottery," *The Nation* 75 (December 25, 1902) : 497.

his protection. From Leslie one learns that Stickney was six feet four; like many others he noted that he "much resembled a Greek god, in spite of his curious staring eyes."[39] Stickney taught Leslie "what was to be said about Oriental China, Japanese script and the Renaissance";[40] and "Greek and French poetry, modern painting and the whole intellectual attitude to life."[41] Other interesting things that one learns from Leslie are that Stickney had a "scheme of ethics and morals" and that he was in love with Gifford Pinchot's sister: "They were both very tall and good-looking, rather like the creatures drawn by George du Maurier in his *Trilby*."[42] Stickney's religious position, which is reflected in his poems, is revealed also by Leslie's comment that "Stickney was a pure pagan and wished to dissuade me against the Catholic Church which fascinated my Sundays."[43]

It is through Leslie that one gets an insight not only into the relationship of three men but also into the development of an important book in our nation's literature:

> In the same *Avenue du Bois de Boulogne* (now called after Foch) lived the wisest and most cynical of Americans, the great Henry Adams. To his feet I was brought by Jo [sic] Stickney and had the sense to listen with a delight which touched the old man. In 1903 he was at his zenith, talking exquisitely about blue China, the modern dynamo, Chartres Cathedral and the Latin mediaeval hymns. His rich personality has been since revealed to a wondering America in his Autobiography. But I knew the book called *The Education of Henry Adams* as conversation. I had only to listen to hear it all while he conversed with Stickney.[44]

39. Shane Leslie, *The Film of Memory* (London: Michael Joseph, Ltd., 1938) , p. 227.
40. *Ibid.*, p. 228.
41. *Ibid., American Wonderland* (London: Michael Joseph, Ltd., 1936) , p. 188.
42. *Ibid.*
43. *Ibid., The Film of Memory*, p. 231.
44. *Ibid.*, p. 229.

Stickney was now nearing the completion of his degree, the *doctorat ès lettres,* which no American before him had received. For it he had written two theses, one in Latin and one in French. The Latin thesis consisted of a life of Ermolao Barbaro (the Younger), fifteenth-century Italian humanist, together with a bibliography and some theretofore unpublished letters, the manuscripts of which Stickney had discovered.[45] The French thesis, much longer than the other, was a study of the clash between rhetoric and suggestive poetic expression in Greek verse.[46] When Stickney went on March 31, 1903, to the Sorbonne to make his oral defense of his work, Leslie went also and recorded his performance in a passage worthy of quoting at length:

> Well I remember the day when he was examined by the French professors, led by Croiset, the Dean, in the Great Hall of the Sorbonne, under the scarlet picture of Richelieu. With what learning and subtlety he defended himself against their sleight of tongue! How they pricked and tore and tossed his thesis! With his beautiful grey eyes[47] and sad, bewildered face he met them on their own ground and in their own tongue! How carelessly the Greek flowed from his lips, and with what unperturbed French he met all their objections for hour after hour. When the strife was over they were all polite congratulations. Although they admitted he was not quite French in his interpretation, they crowned his scholarship.
>
> He was made a Doctor of the Sorbonne *cum summa laude.* . . . When it was all over we made our way under a pale-blue sky to the Avenue du Bois, where old Henry Adams told us all that the Sorbonne could never teach.[48]

45. Trumbull Stickney, *De Hermolai Barbari vita atque ingenio dissertationem* (Paris: *Lutetiae Parisiorum, Société Nouvelle de Librairie et d'Édition,* 1903).

46. *Ibid., Les Sentences dans la Poésie Grecque* (Paris: *Société Nouvelle de Librairie et d'Édition, Librairie Georges Bellais,* 1903). This book will be discussed in chapter 3 along with Stickney's other prose writings.

47. Riggs notes that Stickney's eyes were probably brown, p. 227.

48. Leslie, *American Wonderland,* pp. 187–88.

A further indication of the quality of *Les Sentences* is the fact that it won a medal from *L'Association Pour L'Encouragement des Études Grecques*.[49]

Thus drew to a close the long and rich experience of Paris. Before preparing for home there was another important journey. In the summer of 1903 Stickney spent several weeks in Greece, seeing for the first time the sites of events in Greek literature, many of them out of the way and not well known, that had haunted his imagination. His excitement during this adventure is reflected in the Grecian sonnets it inspired. Stickney returned to Paris and sailed for the United States at the end of August, after making his farewell to Henry Adams and Sylvain Lévi.

At Harvard Stickney showed renewed interest in drama and gave weekly readings from Plato's *Republic*. At first he seemed content, as indicated by a letter to his brother:

> They've given me an easy job if there ever was one, with loads of time to myself. Life is excellent, I find, if you can earn your living and do some things you love, besides seeing the human race, which is good in some ways everywhere.[50]

If his own training had been of a most rigorous kind, it had not warped his perspective as a teacher. E. K. Rand, a colleague, described his work in the classroom:

> His method in teaching was not to present the entire anatomy of a subject, but to arouse enthusiasm for essentials and to develop in detail the problems which awakened immediate interest—a hard method for a plodder, but the only one possible for a genius so vivid as his. Men came to him not for dictation, but for that vitalized information which awakens intelligence. ... He was impressed with the moral and interpretative func-

---

49. See *Revue des Études Grecques* 17 (1904), xxiv–vi.
50. Quoted in Riggs, p. 251, and used here by permission of Mrs. Louise Tanner.

tions of the teacher, the value of his influence on wider circles.[51]

Stickney was thus the master of that extensive training and experience that lay behind him and which in his mind was strengthened and brought to a sharp focus. One can understand Swinburne Hale's observation that it was impossible to be indifferent about him, and probably precisely because of "his sure and persuasive way of expounding the right as he saw it."[52]

Nevertheless, Harvard was not Paris, and there was another side to the picture. Santayana felt that it was a case of "maladaptation":

> I felt that he was forcing himself to play a part, a painful part like that of a convert who tries to live up to his new faith and to forgive his new associates for unintentionally wounding him at every turn. It is tragic in such cases to look back to the lovely familiar world that one has abandoned for being false or wicked, and to seek in vain for compensations and equivalents in the strange system that one has decided to call good and true. So Newman must have suffered when he became a Catholic. When would the ivy mantle these new brick walls, or the voice modulate the Latin liturgy as it had done the English? In some such case I imagined Stickney to find himself, now that he was back in America. His conscience had compelled him to swear allegiance to his country and to his work; but he was not at home; he had always been an exotic, warmed and watered in a greenhouse; and the harsh air and tough weeds of his native heath tried him severely.[53]

One suspects that the passage is overly melodramatic and that it was written to demonstrate a thesis. It must be admitted, however, that a letter from Stickney to his mother, dated December 2, 1903, is in a somewhat similar vein: "A great

51. E. K. Rand, "Joseph Trumbull Stickney," *The Harvard Graduates' Magazine* 13 (December 1904) : 243.
52. Swinburne Hale, "Joseph Trumbull Stickney," *The Harvard Monthly* 39 (December 1904) : 126–27. Hale was then Editor-in-Chief.
53. Santayana, *The Middle Span*, p. 150.

lack of ease benumbs me when I go into the metropolis [Boston]; the simplicity and usages of the older civilizations, and the excitement & brilliancy of the younger here are exquisitely lacking; you're stiff and you're dull."[54]

In the same letter he complained of fatigue. By early spring he had headaches, and his sight and hearing were soon affected. He felt that overwork was the cause of his deteriorating health. By May 12, 1904, he was writing his mother, "There's nothing to get out of life; there are ways to live it."[55] His tendency toward despair was being strengthened by his illness. After the school term he visited his mother, who was staying in New Hampshire, but had to return to Boston for medical attention. It was soon discovered that he had a brain tumor. George Cabot Lodge and his wife and brother came immediately to attend him. According to Moody, "He worked at his poetry almost up to the very end, in spite of severe pain in his head."[56]

Sylvain Lévi was in the United States for a professional meeting and came at once to see Stickney when he heard of his condition. Stickney was now blind and at times unable to walk straight without aid. The doctors feared the results of an emotional scene. Finally they were allowed to meet: As Stickney felt the face he could no longer see he murmured, "O mon papa Sylvain."[57] On October 11, 1904, he was seized with a convulsion and died while still in a coma. He was buried in the family lot at Hartford on October 15. There were a number of eulogies of a personal and official nature. Edwin Arlington Robinson, thinking of the fate of Leopardi,

54. Quoted in Riggs, p. 252, and used here by permission of Mrs. Louise Tanner.
55. Quoted in *Ibid.*, p. 268, and used here by permission of Mrs. Louise Tanner.
56. William Vaughn Moody, *Letters to Harriet*, ed. Percy MacKaye (Boston and New York: Houghton Mifflin Company, 1935), p. 222.
57. *Bhagavad-Gītā*, p. 4.

wrote to Josephine Preston Peabody concerning Stickney, "We could not afford to lose him."[58]

Stickney's literary executors were George Cabot Lodge, John Ellerton Lodge, and William Vaughn Moody. Together they edited *The Poems of Trumbull Stickney*, which was published in 1905 by Houghton Mifflin. Some of Stickney's manuscripts, including a journal of his trip to Greece, a translation of *The Persians* for class use, and the manuscripts that his editors had used for the 1905 edition, disappeared for quite some time. A memoir of Stickney's life by George Cabot Lodge, Stickney's letters to Lodge, Moody, and some other friends, and other materials also disappeared. Riggs drew the conclusion that Stickney's sister Lucy gathered this material for use in writing his biography; she herself died before completing the task, and the material was subsequently lost.[59] However, in 1969 the present writer discovered several translations from the Greek, not all of them complete, and some of the missing manuscripts among materials recently added to the George Cabot Lodge papers at the Massachusetts Historical Society. Lodge's unpublished memoir is also to be found there. Manuscripts used in the preparation of *Dramatic Verses* are at the Houghton Library at Harvard.

Thus passed from the scene at the age of thirty, one who, while not of the first rank of poets, was one of the most accomplished of his own generation and one of the most capable and versatile individuals produced by the period. He was not easily forgotten. In 1907 Moody wrote,

> I dine tonight at the Fletchers' (Herrick's brother-in-law) to meet a friend of Joe's, who has expressed a desire to see me on that score. Nearly every week I encounter a similar example of the hold Joe had taken upon the affections of the men who knew him, and the tacit free-masonry which his memory creates

---

58. Neff, p. 135.
59. For Riggs's discussion of Stickney's papers see p. 275 and pp. 284–86.

among all such. That is what you call, and what I am willing to call with you, success in life.[60]

Moody dreaded returning to a Paris without Trumbull Stickney.[61]

The blow fell hardest on George Cabot Lodge, who was himself to die in August of 1909. Lodge wrote twenty-six sonnets as an elegy to his friend and published them in *The Great Adventure*. Perhaps the following octave and sonnet best capture the spirit of Stickney:

> "At least," he said, "we spent with Socrates
>   Some memorable days, and in our youth
>   Were curious and respectful of the Truth,
>   Thrilled with perfections and discoveries.
> And with the everlasting mysteries
>   We were irreverent and unsatisfied,—
>   And so we are!" he said. . . .
>
> He said: "We are the Great Adventurers,
>   This is the Great Adventure: thus to be
>   Alive and, on the universal sea
>   Of being, lone yet dauntless mariners.
> In the rapt outlook of astronomers
>   To rise thro' constellated gyres of thought;
>   To fall with shattered pinions, overwrought
>   With flight, like unrecorded Lucifers:—
> Thus to receive identity, and thus
>   Return at last to the dark element,—
>   This is the Great Adventure!" All of us,
> Who saw his dead, deep-visioned eyes, could see,
>   After the Great Adventure, immanent,
>   Splendid and strange, the Great Discovery![62]

---

60. Moody, *Letters to Harriet,* p. 325.
61. *Ibid.,* p. 337.
62. *Poems and Dramas of George Cabot Lodge* (Boston and New York: Houghton Mifflin Company, 1911), 2: 69–70.

In Paris Henry Adams felt the loss deeply and wrote George Cabot Lodge in November of 1905,

> I am sure that Joe is pleased at your *in memoriam,* as he may well be. I have sought with microscopes and megaphones for another to take his place, but the Latin Quarter swarms without use for my fishing.[63]

---

63. Quoted in Riggs, p. 280, and used here by permission of George Cabot Lodge.

2

Fin de Siècle and the Harvard Poets

Looking back on the literary scene of the 1890s, one can now see that it was a period of transition between the old and the new. Our concern here is not with the prose writers who, like Stephen Crane, had hardly more than begun what seemed a brilliant career, only to have death claim them; but in the final analysis Crane's career strangely parallels that of many of the poets who began publishing during the same period.

There were of course some survivors of the older tradition of New England letters: James Russell Lowell (d. 1891), Oliver Wendell Holmes (d. 1894), and John Greenleaf Whittier (d. 1892). It can be no surprise that these patriarchs were said by the less worshipful to be "running in grooves." It proved difficult to find their successors, especially since Walt Whitman and Emily Dickinson had to wait until time caught up with them.

James Whitcomb Riley gave the masses what they wanted and was rewarded accordingly. Indeed, the sugary sentimentalism associated with children, one's own childhood, and the bygone past of youth had been widely popular for some time and had been amusingly satirized by Mark Twain in *Adventures of Huckleberry Finn,* especially in the "Ode to Stephen Dowling Bots, Dec'd." In *Poems* (1894) and *Lyrics* (1897), Father Tabb displayed both the devotion and wit of an earlier period. Much was expected of Madison Cawein (1865–1914), the Kentucky poet who worked as a pool-hall cashier and was loudly praised by William Dean Howells for his poetic achievements. The nature poems that Howells preferred are likely to strike the modern reader as lame indeed when compared to Cawein's stark, almost impressionistic technique in such regional pieces as "Lynchers," "Feud," "Ku Klux," and "The Man Hunt." The first of these ends with a brief symbolic setting, repeated from the beginning, that is perfectly consonant with the violence of the act:

> An oath, a shuffle; a ring of masks;
> A voice that answers a voice that asks.
>
> A group of shadows; the moon's red fleck;
> A running noose and a man's bared neck.
>
> A word, a curse, and a shape that swings;
> The lonely night and a bat's black wings.
>
> At the moon's down-going let it be
> On the quarry hill with its one gnarled tree.[1]

One cannot help but feel that Cawein would have retained a better reputation if he had written more poems in this vein. Richard Hovey joined with the Canadian Bliss Carman to produce *Songs from Vagabondia* (1894), which begins:

---

1. Madison Cawein, *Poems* (New York: The Macmillan Company, 1911), pp. 217–18.

> Off with the fetters
> That chafe and restrain!
> Off with the chain!
> Here Art and Letters,
> Music and wine,
> And Myrtle and Wanda,
> The winsome witches,
> Blithely combine.[2]

Further reading confirms the impression that one perhaps gets from these lines, that the authors seek the sensationalism of Whitman's spirit of rebellion while being careful not to go too far. For the really genteel there was the sanctified verse of Henry van Dyke (1852–1933), who lived long enough to oppose the real revolution in American poetry after the turn of the century and who defined poetry as "idealism set to music."[3]

For the more gifted and determined young poets it was far from an auspicious time to begin a career. Larzer Ziff considers the failure of Stickney, Lodge, and Moody to break through to a really new style to be the result of "a stalemate of two traditions—that of Whitman and that of Victorian English verse—whose conflicts rendered their inheritors powerless to find a way out of the twilight time."[4] There were many such cross currents to contend with. In his study of the period Carlin T. Kindilien considers much of the poetry to be in the genteel tradition: "In their worship of the past, their fondness for historical myth and legend, their addiction to the exotic and the picturesque, and especially in their peculiar combination of the ideal, the spiritual, and the didac-

---

2. *Songs from Vagabondia* (Boston: Small, Maynard and Company, 1907), p. 1.
3. Quoted in *The Literature of the American People,* ed. Arthur Hobson Quinn (New York: Appleton-Century-Crofts, Inc., 1951), p. 726.
4. Larzer Ziff, *The American 1890s, Life and Times of a Lost Generation* (New York: The Viking Press, 1966), p. 314.

tic, these poets of the Nineties manifested many of the qualities of genteelism."[5] From the days of Grant through 1900 there was a very considerable amount of verse protesting the evils that accompanied the shift to an industrial society, especially the worship of Mammon, crooked politicians, and the grim life of the worker. But the very power this materialism yielded resulted in an overwhelming amount of poetry exalting America as a country with a unique role to play in the course of the world's events as a result of God's or destiny's scheme of things.[6] In the face of all this, one wonders why the mask of the clown, which Jules Laforgue in France had found amusing and which T. S. Eliot later wore, was not tried on more often; Moody showed briefly what it could do in "The Menagerie" (1900). Experiments with the *persona* of the poet were to be one of the most conspicuous features of the poetic revolution when it finally came. Another source of that revolution's power, a conscious appeal to folk elements, was effectively blocked. Louise Bogan notes that "the energy of folk poetry was, however, at this time [about 1900] and for years to come, rigidly separated from the formal poetry of the period by barriers of taste."[7]

One of the greatest problems lay in the area of critical canons, which denied the vitality poetry needed in order to catch up with the rapid advances prose had made. Such critic-poets as Richard Henry Stoddard (1825–1903), Bayard Taylor (1825–1878), George Henry Boker (1823–1890), Thomas Bailey Aldrich (1836–1907), and Edmund Clarence

---

5. Carlin T. Kindilien, *American Poetry in the Eighteen Nineties* (Providence, R. I.: Brown University Press, 1956), p. 30.

6. A detailed treatment of social awareness in verse of the period is Robert H. Walker, *The Poet and the Gilded Age, Social Themes in Late 19th Century American Verse* (Philadelphia: University of Pennsylvania Press, 1963).

7. Louise Bogan, *Achievement in American Poetry 1900–1950* (Chicago: Henry Regnery Company, 1951), p. 4.

Stedman (1833–1908) had defended what Willard Thorp calls "Ideality":

> From the time of the Civil War until past the turn of the century, the writing and the criticism of poetry were largely in the hands of a group of friends bound by many personal and literary ties. Presenting a united front to the materialism of the age, resentful of the claims of the realists, they self-consciously proclaimed themselves the champions of Ideality in literature. Their influence was so persuasive that when their control over editors and publishers was broken by the writers of the newer generation, the naturalistic revolt was the more violent because they had held it in check for more than a quarter of a century.[8]

Thorp goes on to state,

> The aesthetic aims of the group explain in part such features of their humanism as their excessive idolization of the artist and the decline in their poetry of the earlier romantic enthusiasm for nature. The ideal world of the poet is not revealed to him by contact with nature; it is not the natural world transformed. It obeys its own laws, which are aesthetic.[9]

Taking this concept from Professor Thorp, one notices that it is similar in important ways to literary movements in France and England. The movement called Symbolism was well under way in France. Its characteristics are summarized by Bruce Weirick as follows:

> The theory of these [French] poets is that only in symbols is there truth, beauty, and happiness. Life thus becomes an effort to disregard reality, and to live in the land of dreams, or perhaps to regard reality as itself a land of dreams. . . . To arouse the mystical consciousness, and to use reality or passion or friendship only as the symbol to lead them into the right and visionary state, is the purpose of the poems and plays and novels of the Symbolists.[10]

---

8. Willard Thorp, "Defenders of Ideality," in *Literary History of the United States: History,* ed. Robert E. Spiller *et al* (New York: The Macmillan Company, 1963) , p. 809.

9. *Ibid.,* p. 814.

10. Bruce Weirick, *From Whitman to Sandburg in American Poetry* (New York: The Macmillan Company, 1924) , pp. 110–11.

This theory was to result in some fine poetry in France; it is obviously different from Ideality, primarily because of the metaphysics of the Symbol. However, the orientation toward a dream world marks both movements, and the lethargy proved the more compelling in America.

Turning to England one finds a somewhat similar phenomenon in William Butler Yeats and the tragic generation of the Rhymers' Club (formed in 1891), some of whom wrote reviews for *The Yellow Book* and *The Savoy*.[11] The members included Ernest Dowson, Victor Plarr, Richard Le Gallienne, Aubrey Beardsley, John Davidson, Lionel Johnson, Arthur Symons, and Ernest Rhys, all of whom admired Dante Gabriel Rossetti and Walter Pater. They claimed Catullus and Herrick as masters but wrote their own melancholic verse. To compare this movement with those in America and France, one has only to look at two of the finest poems of the two best poets of the group (excluding Yeats, whose poetry of Faeryland of the time is another example): Lionel Johnson's "By the Statue of King Charles at Charing Cross" and Ernest Dowson's "Nuns of the Perpetual Adoration." The composite image that emerges from these two poems is one of stasis: though a symbol of the martyr's triumph, the statue of Charles points to a spirit beyond time, while the nuns, though in tune with the infinite, have safely withdrawn from the world.

It took only a slight shift to combine melancholy and the world of dreams by placing the latter in the past, as a great many poems of the period will attest, including A. E. Housman's "Into my heart an air that kills," where it becomes "the land of lost content." Accompanying this trend in America was a readiness to use myth in a new way, one that the

---

11. A pointed discussion may be found in Richard Ellmann, *Yeats: The Man and the Masks* (New York: The Macmillan Company, 1948), pp. 140–41.

twentieth century would find quite fruitful. Kindilien notes that "the verse dramas of Hovey and Moody and the long poems of Robinson were soon to reflect the American poets' growing appreciation of the medieval and classical myths and allegories as structures for the themes of the modern world."[12] One may object that the result was not a fortunate one, as Edmund Wilson seems to do, when, speaking of Moody and Stickney, he says, "the appetite is baffled by the peculiar aridities of the aesthetic American of the nineties, who combines sensuous imagery and sighing emotions with a medium which, for all his efforts, remains basically rocklike and cold, who ransacks the recorded passions of classical antiquity or Renaissance Italy to find only frustrations appropriate to a novel by Henry James or Edith Wharton."[13] Mr. Wilson, who has consistently praised Stickney's other verse, implies that this attempt to use the past proved a failure. However, some of Stickney's most memorable lines appear in such verse, and one senses that it was proving to be valuable training in terms of pure craftsmanship. Certainly the work of Lodge, Moody, and Stickney in this area foreshadowed Eliot's greater success in the same tradition.[14]

When the revolution did come it found a multitude of criteria to justify itself, as the labels "Imagism," "Objectivism," "Vorticism," and the like indicate. Once freed of older critical standards, poets began conducting technical experiments, which parallel the experiments in other art forms,

---

12. Kindilien, p. 77.

13. Edmund Wilson, "The Country I Remember," *The New Republic* 103 (October 14, 1940): 529.

14. Van Wyck Brooks notes that "in the revolt against New England that marked the nation's coming of age, the New England authors were almost totally ignored. The Yankee classics were dethroned, and the critics scarcely mentioned such authors as Miss Guiney, Lodge and Stickney. . . . One had to pay for being a Yankee in these great formative years of the national mind." *New England: Indian Summer, 1865–1915* (New York: E. P. Dutton & Co., Inc., 1940), p. 509 n.

with syntax, sound, image, and rhythm. Poetry had at last caught up with the other arts. The interval between the old and the new, when the poets of the 90s were at work, is a period that has received little attention until recently. A considerable chasm exists in the tradition from the Brahmins to the Imagists, and the unique careers of Whitman and Dickinson do not bridge it. An examination of the Harvard poets at the end of the century will cast some light upon the problems facing the poet of that time, his methods of dealing with them, and how he anticipated the achievements of the next few decades.

As an outsider looking in, Edwin Arlington Robinson offers a valuable perspective on Harvard in the 90s as it was seen by a poet who later achieved distinction by making something new of basically traditional verse. The year he was a special student he wrote to Arthur R. Gledhill,

> I feel as if I had always been here, and as if I should always like to stay here. If there is any class of people in the world that I envy, they are the Freshmen, who have four years of Harvard life before them instead of eight months. However, I am not growling, but consider myself fortunate as it is. I "sprung" a ballade on the *Advocate* a while ago. Much to my surprise, it was accepted.[15]

As has already been mentioned, he was to have no success with the more prestigious *Monthly* during his stay. Two years later, back in Gardiner, Maine, Robinson wrote Gledhill again of the experience: "I am a better man with better ideals than I was before I went, but I am afraid they are not

---

15. *Selected Letters of Edwin Arlington Robinson* (New York: The Macmillan Company, 1940), p. 7.

the ideals to help me in the active walk of life, whatever they may be."[16]

Harvard was a place of retreat for a young writer, with both the advantages and dangers of such an existence. Santayana saw it in somewhat the same light when in 1936 he wrote William Lyon Phelps regarding *The Last Puritan:*

> An important element in the *tragedy* of Oliver (not in his personality, for he was no poet) is drawn from the fate of a whole string of Harvard poets in the 1880's and 1890's—Sanborn, Philip Savage, Hugh McCullough [sic], Trumbull Stickney, and Cabot Lodge: also Moody, although he lived a little longer and made some impression, I believe, as a playwright. Now all those friends of mine, Stickney especially, of whom I was very fond, were visibly killed by the lack of air to breathe. People individually were kind and appreciative to them, as they were to me; but the system was deadly, and they hadn't any alternative tradition (as I had) to fall back upon: and of course, as I believe I said of Oliver in my letter, they hadn't the strength of a great intellectual hero who can stand alone.[17]

Santayana knew what he was talking about, because he had felt the pressure himself. In an episode that strangely foreshadows the Conservative Christian Anarchists society of Lodge, Stickney, and Adams in Paris, Santayana was involved in 1892 with the Laodicean Club. In his autobiography Robert Morss Lovett calls the Club "partly a joke, designed to *épater* the Cambridge bourgeoisie, partly a reassertion of the traditional Harvard indifference."[18] The name of the group suggests God's judgment upon the church of Laodicea: "So then because thou art lukewarm, and neither cold nor hot, I will spue thee out of my mouth" (Revelation 3:16). The Club met in Lovett's rooms and included Santayana,

---

16. *Ibid.,* p. 10.

17. *The Letters of George Santayana*, ed. Daniel Cory (New York: Charles Scribner's Sons, 1955), p. 306.

18. *All Our Years* (New York: The Viking Press, 1948), p. 46.

Norman and Hutchins Hapgood, W. F. Harris, Arthur S. Hayes, and several others. Santayana was elected pope, and while canonizing the saints of Laodicea the members proposed Horace, Goethe, and Omar Khayyám. Lovett favored Lucrezia Borgia for virgin, because she "exercised a wise indifference in difficult circumstances," while Santayana favored God.

> Since the Laodiceans could not be enthusiastic even about their church, it was the rule that if at any meeting a quorum should be present the club should *ipso facto* cease to exist. As a result, the second meeting was the last.[19]

Like the Conservative Christian Anarchists, the Laodicean Club shows something of the pressures upon those who originated it. This same pressure is revealed in Santayana's neoplatonic sonnets of the 80s and 90s in which "the spirit dwelling in her clay" wishes to be free of the restrictions and limitations of man's lot, to "shed the flesh awhile, becoming mind."[20] In his own career at Harvard Santayana thus foreshadowed the fate of those he later described. If he himself escaped it, it was by leaving poetry for philosophy and America for Europe.

An important outlet for young writers, though not available to all, as both Robinson and Lodge were to find, was *The Harvard Monthly*. Norman Hapgood, a former editor-in-chief wise enough to change the rules to allow Moody to publish as a freshman, gives an admirable sketch of the magazine and those associated with it:

> I have no hesitation in saying there has never been in America an undergraduate publication to approach it. This standard was partly, but only in part, due to the contributions from

19. *Ibid.*
20. George Santayana, *The Poet's Testament* (New York: Charles Scribner's Sons, 1953), p. 11.

alumni, usually one in each issue. George R. Carpenter, afterward professor at Columbia, was a young instructor when he gave us the first translation in English of Ibsen's *Lady From The Sea*. Santayana also was a young instructor when he gave us some of his loveliest poetry, and such prose pieces as his dialogue on the qualities of Walt Whitman. But most of what gave to this magazine its splendid quality was undergraduate. Alan Houghton, afterward member of Congress and ambassador to Germany and Great Britain, was the first editor-in-chief, a few years before my time on the periodical, and among the early editors were Bernhard [*sic*] Berenson, the art critic, and the Boston editor and author, Mark A. de W. Howe. Robert Herrick the novelist followed me as editor-in-chief. . . . Another close friend was Robert Morss Lovett, editor-in-chief two years after me.[21]

Not only did the *Monthly* provide an opportunity for publication; it also, in reviews and essays, provided a forum for discussion of specific poets and poetry in general. Anyone glancing at its faded pages today is likely to agree with Hapgood's evaluation of the magazine.

One of the founders of the *Monthly* was Thomas Parker Sanborn, class of '86. He was also a co-editor of the *Lampoon,* which published his light verse. After graduation he turned to journalism and published in *Life* and the Springfield *Republican,* of which he was assistant editor. Extremely sensitive, and perhaps paranoid, judging from Santayana's obituary for him in the *Monthly* in 1889, Sanborn took his own life. He was thus the first of the list of these poets who died young. Another poet and early editor of the magazine was Henry Shelton Sanford, class of '88. Sanford was devoted to literature, knew the Latin classics well, and was playfully cynical. He published in *Scribner's* and other periodicals after graduation, but soon suffered from bad health. Ironically, perhaps his best poem is "Ode to Death," published

21. Norman Hapgood, *The Changing Years* (New York: Farrar & Rinehart, Inc., 1930) , pp. 76–77.

in the *Monthly* in 1886. Houghton, Sanford, Sanborn, and Santayana were members of a group called the "Harvard Pessimists."[22]

More talented than either Sanborn or Sanford was Philip Henry Savage, class of '93. Savage was born in 1868 but did not enter Harvard until 1889, because he was occupied for three years prior to that as a drummer of boots and shoes. His letters home discussed business and described nature, into whose service he was drawn as a sensitive observer, almost a delicate one. A special student in 1891–92, he helped edit *The Mahogany Tree* and took two of Stickney's poems[23] in the spring. Savage's father was a Unitarian minister, and so it was natural that his son should enter the Divinity School after graduation. He soon left it, however, for the English Department and a master's degree. Savage taught for a few years but spent the last three years of his life as secretary to the Librarian of the Boston Public Library. During this period he published *First Poems and Fragments* in 1895 and *Poems* in 1898. On June 4, 1899, Savage died, less than a week after he had been stricken with appendicitis. His friend Daniel Gregory Mason edited his poems after his death.[24]

Savage loved nature and resented man's desolation of its charms, since "where man has conquered nature dies." In addition, he was fond of brief, well-chiseled pieces such as "The Water-Clock":

> Ever with fainter pulse and throw
> The heart's red clepsydra will flow.
> Then lest the drops run on to waste,
> Make haste, for love of life, make haste!

22. For a discussion of this group and its relation to Schopenhauer, see Maurice Fred Brown, Jr., *Harvard Poetic Renaissance: 1885–1910* (Harvard dissertation, 1958), pp. 156–57.

23. Stickney's poetry will be discussed in detail in chapters 5–7.

24. *The Poems of Philip Henry Savage* (Boston: Small, Maynard, and Company, 1901).

Nature is the concern of most of the poems, but the minister's son evidently had doubts in regard to its Creator. Certainly this is the suggestion of the poem beginning:

> God, thou art good, but not to me.
> Some dark, some high and holier plan
> Is hid beyond the world with thee.
> To the immortals, not to man,
> God, thou art good.

Even more bitter is the posthumous poem that has as its first two stanzas the following:

> What hard, bright Spirit sits beyond the stars,
> On what high seat beyond the round of space?
> With what benignant, what pernicious face
> Views he the blood, the laughter, and the scars?
>
> We may not reach beyond our prison bars.
> He will not bend to touch us in our place.
> We can but lift our heads and strive to trace
> His handiwork in what he makes or mars.

These protests and the terse elegiac pieces will probably strike the modern reader as having more life than the derivative nature poems.[25]

Hugh McCulloch, class of '94, was a poet with different loyalties. Influenced by the Pre-Raphaelites and the decadents, he published *The Quest of Herakles and Other Poems* in 1894; the design was by Pierre La Rose, class of '95. Using French forms with some skill, McCulloch published in the *Monthly* and tended to combine classical subjects with *fin de siècle* attitudes. He died in Florence in 1902.

---

25. Riggs asserts that "the strength of Savage's poetry is the strength of an older tradition—the tradition of Emerson and Thoreau—and of the time before American letters had been emasculated by the genteel tradition, before the Brahmins had established the separation of the spirit from its physical basis." P. 50 (see chap. 1, n. 1). I am indebted to Riggs for details concerning the more obscure Harvard poets.

Poets were many and varied at Harvard. Daniel Gregory Mason records his meeting with one of the more successful. Mason and La Rose occasionally dined at a restaurant near Harvard Square mostly frequented by the poorer students:

> One evening in the spring of our junior year la Rose recognized there an old school friend, a man of middle stature, full-blooded complexion, and studious air, whose deep liquid blue eyes seemed to look through appearances into essences. His manner was reserved but friendly. We fell into talk, or at least la Rose and I did, while his friend smoked a pipe ponderingly, pressing it with thoughtful forefinger, and from time to time dropped brief comments, often hardly more than resonant ejaculations. . . . Unusual, too, seemed to me his dress: both florid and careless, as if a barbaric taste for magnificence in waistcoats and neckties found itself unsupported by an attention that was set on things more worth while. Most of our friends were trim with a New England trimness; this man breathed the freshness, almost uncouth, of the West. Yet his unconventionality, far from seeming eccentric, was delightfully friendly and intimate.[26]

The new acquaintance was William Vaughn Moody, whose success with the *Monthly* has already been discussed. The Middle ages furnished much of his subject matter and perhaps inspired the frequent archaisms. Stickney's association with Moody proved valuable, for, as one of Moody's critics says,

> He was an excellent classical scholar when he went up to Harvard. But for his later and deeper interest in Greek literature he was largely indebted to Trumbull Stickney, whose influence upon him Moody rated high, and whose untimely death affected him greatly.[27]

26. Daniel Gregory Mason, *Music in My Time* (New York: The Macmillan Company, 1938) , p. 21.

27. *The Poems and Plays of William Vaughn Moody,* with an introduction by John M. Manly (Boston and New York: Houghton Mifflin Company, 1912) , 1: xxxi.

George Cabot Lodge had no success with the *Monthly,* but no doubt the Harvard experience left its mark on him. Inclined to philosophy, by the time he got to Paris his views on time itself were developed to the point where tragedy was probably inevitable:

> The past is like a great pit, and the present like a frittered edge which is continually crumbling and falling utterly down into the pit. . . . And the future—it is the veriest of common-places to say the future doesn't exist. It is nothing but a prob-ability—at best a hope.[28]

It was in Paris that Lodge tried to free himself from his Bostonian origins. His association with the Conservative Christian Anarchists has already been noted. Cater describes the appearance of the young rebel in Paris:

> he wore a large black hat that had the dimensions of a sombrero; a fine gold watch chain that he inherited from his grandfather hung around his neck and the rest of it was draped on the front of his vest. He affected a kind of leonine look and manner. With this habit of dress, along with his passion for living and love of beauty in every form, he became the poet incarnate. Some people were repelled, others were fascinated.[29]

But the *persona* disintegrated with the advent of the Spanish-American War, even after the stay in Berlin and the study of Schopenhauer. Boston claimed its own. Lodge's publications included *The Song of the Wave* (1898), *Poems* (1902), *Cain* (1904), *The Great Adventure* (1905), *Herakles* (1908), and *The Soul's Inheritance* (1909).

The will that valiantly strives for achievement in the face of an uncaring universe is symbolized in the title poem of *The Song of the Wave:*

---

28. Letter of April 5, 1896. Quoted in *The Life of George Cabot Lodge* by Henry Adams (Boston and New York: Houghton Mifflin Company, 1911), pp. 42–43.

29. Harold Dean Cater, ed., *Henry Adams and His Friends* (Boston: Houghton Mifflin Company, 1947), p. lxxxii.

> This is the song of the wave, that died in the
>   fulness of life.
> The prodigal this, that lavished its largess of
>   strength
>   In the lust of attainment.
> Aiming at things for Heaven too high,
> Sure in the pride of life, in the richness of strength.
> So tried it the impossible height, till the end was
>   found:
> Where ends the soul that yearns for the fillet of
>   morning stars,
> The soul in the toils of the journeying worlds,
> Whose eye is filled with the Image of God,
>   And the end is Death![30]

Elizabeth Stevenson has compared Lodge's work with Stickney's:

> Stickney's gift was curiously opposite to his friend's. Lodge's
> focus was idea; Stickney's, emotion. Lodge's aim was a defini-
> tion of belief; Stickney's, an attainment of a state of being.
> Lodge's tone was cool; Stickney's, warm.[31]

The first significant, and the best, critic of Lodge's work, though a partial one, was his friend Henry Adams. Adams was especially intrigued by the dramas:

> Lodge's dramatic motive was always the same, whether in
> "Cain," or in "Herakles," or in the minor poems. It was that of
> Schopenhauer, of Buddhism, of Oriental thought everywhere,—
> the idea of Will, making the universe, but existing only as sub-
> ject. The Will is God; it is nature; it is all that is; but it is
> knowable only as ourself. Thus the sole tragic action of hu-
> manity is the Ego,—the Me,—always maddened by the necessity
> of self-sacrifice, the superhuman effort of lifting himself and

---

30. *Poems and Dramas of George Cabot Lodge* (Boston and New York: Houghton Mifflin Company, 1911), 1: 9.

31. Elizabeth Stevenson, *Henry Adams* (New York: The Macmillan Company, 1955), p. 298.

the universe by sacrifice, and, of course, by destroying the attachments which are most vital, in order to attain.[32]

Adams read Lodge's career as an allegory illustrating his notion of a devitalized civilization. A month after the poet's death he wrote Henry James,

> Bay Lodge's experience last winter completed and finished my own. When his *Herakles* appeared absolutely unnoticed by the literary press, I regarded my thesis as demonstrated. Society no longer shows the intellectual life necessary to enable it to react against a stimulus. My brother Brooks insists on the figure of paralysis. I prefer the figure of diffusion.[33]

In the biography of two years later Adams returned to the subject:

> Society was not disposed to defend itself from criticism or attack. Indeed, the most fatal part of the situation for the poet in revolt, the paralyzing drug that made him helpless, was that society no longer seemed sincerely to believe in itself or anything else; it resented nothing, not even praise. The young poet grew up without being able to find an enemy.[34]

Such, then, was the group of poets that was produced by Harvard in the 80s and 90s. Maurice F. Brown, Jr., has divided them into camps, calling Santayana, McCulloch, and Stickney "aesthetes"; and Lodge, Moody, and to some degree Savage, "pagans" and "primitivists":

> The poetic theory of the Harvard aesthetes and that of the Harvard pagans balance each other in almost perfect antithesis. If the fundamental criterion for the aesthetes in both life and

---

32. *The Life of George Cabot Lodge*, pp. 109–10.
33. *Letters of Henry Adams* (1892–1918), ed. Worthington Chauncey Ford (Boston and New York: Houghton Mifflin Company, 1938), p. 522.
34. *The Life of George Cabot Lodge*, p. 17. Jay Martin has called this biography "perhaps the first piece of literary criticism in which the isolation of the twentieth-century artist is the central principle." *Harvests of Change, American Literature 1865–1914* (Englewood Cliffs, N. J.: Prentice-Hall, Inc., 1967), p. 296.

poetry was structure, that of the pagans was vitality. They preferred the rich welter of immediate experience to the control of form, passionate strife to peace, and the indefinite and intense experience to the clearly-defined and intelligible one. Their poetry is a poetry of energy and strenuous becoming, not one of static perfection and being. In effect, the Harvard pagans accepted the aesthetic principles that Santayana most vigorously rejected in *The Sense of Beauty*.[35]

Such generalizations may be useful, but one should remember that, of all humans, poets are the most inclined toward individuality and uniqueness. And the impression one is finally left with after studying these poets is that, despite their short lives and limited success, they represent a variety and vitality almost in opposition to their time. Perhaps that was part of the problem, for Malcolm Cowley links them with another and later Harvard product, T. S. Eliot:

who himself started writing in the tradition of the forgotten Harvard poets of the 1890s, with their Greek learning, their mixture of paganism and Catholicism, their desire to achieve French worldliness, and their belief that poetic dramas are the highest form of literature. Eliot wrote the poems they had all tried to write; he even mastered the poetic drama, in which they had all failed. In the 1950s a battalion or two of little Eliots were trying to realize, for a second time, the frustrated dreams of Philip Henry Savage, Cabot Lodge, and Trumbull Stickney, whose names they had scarcely heard.[36]

---

35. *Harvard Poetic Renaissance: 1885–1910* (Harvard dissertation, 1958), p. 225. Quoted by permission of Professor Brown.
36. Malcolm Cowley, *The Literary Situation* (New York: The Viking Press, 1954), p. 244.

3

Fiction, Essays, and Criticism

Trumbull Stickney's prose has received very little attention. This prose consists of critical articles, literary essays, and brief fiction; it is for the most part interesting in its own right and also helps to reveal the attitudes and opinions of the man who wrote the poetry, the primary object of our concern. The reader of this poetry will find that Stickney's prose offers another perspective for understanding the verse.

The fiction consists of three short stories, two of moderate length and one rather brief one. In general, Stickney's fiction is concerned with character analysis in contrast to a plot based upon action, and it is written in a style that recalls Henry James in its versatility and flexibility; there is, however, little of James's tendency toward extreme verbosity. The style of the fiction is slightly more restrained than that of the other prose, and it bears the marks of apprenticeship.

"Matters of Circumstance"[1] was printed when Stickney had just reached the age of twenty. The story concerns Mr.

---

1. *The Harvard Monthly* 18 (June 1894) : 147-67.

Catch, a Wall Street man, and his socially ambitious and dominating wife, Adelaide. Mr. Catch, after fifteen years in his position, suffers from "nervous prostration," and the family, including the daughter Edith, seventeen at the opening of the story, sails for Florence, which "has become a world of Anglo-American exiles, who have fled their ill-health, reputation, poverty or ennui, and there warm over the cold dishes of a once excited life." There Mr. Catch survives for two years before expiring. His warm and gentle daughter has been his chief comfort. Before very long, Arthur Courtnay, a twenty-eight-year-old American who has been in Europe for some time, enters the scene. Mrs. Catch, now thirty-eight and still attractive, is fascinated by the sophisticated Courtnay and falls in love with him. He enjoys the company of Mrs. Catch and Edith and is ready to settle down. Soon they are married, and Adelaide gives Courtnay the passionate affection she had never felt for Mr. Catch. During a period when Adelaide is stricken with Roman fever, Courtnay and Edith are thrown more and more in each other's company. They slowly realize that the marriage was a mistake: that it is they who are in love. The situation being an impossible one, Edith decides to escape by marrying "Gordon" (heretofore unmentioned), telling Courtnay, "I shall be yours somewhere, my darling."

An important stylistic feature of this story is a series of generalizations sprinkled throughout that resemble classical *sententiae*. Most of these are abstract statements; some are tied specifically to persons or places: "love and mastery are in women precise opposites—a woman either loves or tyrannizes"; "Courtnay had that peculiar indifference and nonchalance that is so attractive to women"; "It seems probable that what makes all men live on is the hope of change"; "And artistic interests have this advantage, that even to the weakest, there are times when it seems possible to scale the heights —the old mirage of art!"; "Still the best things of life, among others life itself, grow monotonous"; "Yet necessity is a genial force; it is the oil that enables life to run on so long"; "It is very probable that all love is a matter of circumstance"; "Who shall set a standard to apply equally at the crises, the beginnings, the calms, the terrors of life? Who shall venture to judge a madman, or to price his reward?"—and, comparing the problems of modern man with those of monks during the Middle Ages, with their intricate systems of logic to aid them, Courtnay says, "Just think of our mistakes! They are like veins in the marble of being."

"A Dull Study"[2] deals with a poet who is destroyed by wealth and social success. Ralph Egerton is a young poet who has not attempted to publish: "Because he wanted a start. It was his idea to get ease and encouragement,—they were necessary, the conditions for producing good verse being a luxuriousness of life." He also desires

a life of travel and large possibilities. To see the world—wasn't that the *sine qua non* of good writing? One can write well only of what one has experienced; one must experience; how can one get experience?

Money is the answer, or so Egerton thinks; accordingly, he marries an heiress, for whom he feels no deep affection:

The problem was a nasty one—life-interest against soul-interest, and on the face of it might appear easy of solution. But life-interests are fickle sophists and exorcise the soul. Nor was the situation any the easier for his being, as one might say, an artist, imbued with knowledge of the ideal and love of emotional truth. For he was merely a promising young poet.

But after the marriage his plans do not succeed. His writing

---

2. *Ibid.* 19 (January 1895) : 162-68.

worsens. In desperation he sends a short novel written several years earlier to a publisher; it is accepted and praised among Egerton's society friends. His ruin is assured. The conflict between vanity and frustration drives him to drink, and the story ends with his being carried home intoxicated from his Club. "A Dull Study" is a tentative probing of the relationship between an author and an affluent society, a theme which Hemingway was to treat so well in "The Snows of Kilimanjaro."

"Dead-Levels"[3] is the least successful of the three pieces of fiction. It concerns Mary Caldwell, her fiancé Ralph Ainger, and their friend Jack Gherardy. Ralph buries himself in his work and preaches earnestness and sincerity; in reality he is hiding from life, protecting himself from the knowledge of his social inadequacy. Jack is a man of little ambition but with many friends and a considerable knowledge of the world. In the end Mary chooses Jack, rejecting Ralph, whose life is "cooped up in the four walls of moral prejudice" with its "crude ideals." Perhaps the story indicates Stickney's increasing desire for freedom and wider experience, which Paris was eventually to provide.

Stickney's criticism and essays are more successful than his fiction. They reveal a precociousness that is joyous in its own powers of perception and in its readiness to bring to any work a richness of literary experience that allows for a catholicity of taste. Above all there is a desire to praise, as well as to blame, to judge the work on its own merits, not according to a narrow and preconceived standard.

The first essay, appearing as early as January of 1893, is a delightfully urbane piece entitled "Pliny and Letter-Writing."[4] Stickney begins by quoting from critics who have at-

---

3. *Ibid.* 20 (April 1895) : 57–68.
4. *Ibid.* 15 (January 1893) : 147–53.

tacked Pliny's character, especially his supposed egotism.
Such criticism is irrelevant: "Of the literary merit of the
letters we have learned nothing. Might it not be that the
value of correspondence is just that revelation of character
which enables our critics so sharply to blame the writer?"
He then turns to an analysis of this character. Admittedly,
Pliny was an egoist and made no attempt to conceal it; but
he would not have understood our objection, for we have
been taught to suppress the self in conformity to a modern
code: "It becomes natural to us to curb emotion generally,
and, just as we have been taught to avoid the self in conversa-
tion, so in our inner life constantly to be struggling against
the subtlety of self-evaluation." It was not so in the past:

> But in the ancient world, if anything can be asserted so broadly,
> we find that first and last the individual was the unit of life. To
> play his important part he had time to develop—and that to
> the utmost—his peculiar personal character. For this he re-
> quired to find expression for every impulse—not expression
> alone, but easy, fluent translation of thought into something
> tangible, palpable. Every thought had a right to its word and
> gesture; and if he was, as every man must constantly be, con-
> cerned with himself, his reflections were here as worthy of
> expression as any others.

Thus when a modern reader finds a classical writer egotistical,
he must "always make large allowance for this prejudice of
ours, keeping constantly in mind that while the end of our
education is the broader interest of society, the end of theirs
was the perfection of the individual through his emotions."
Stickney continues with a discussion of *otium*, the "leisure"
one can scarcely comprehend today but which was necessary
to produce the kind of letters Pliny wrote. Having little real
leisure, one writes terse, impersonal business letters or in-
tensely personal ones to the few with whom he is closest.
Neither type comes close to Pliny's civility: "So that letter-

writing then was more of an open diary, a ready means of expressing what was uppermost in the writer's mind." What one should "most value in a correspondence of those times" is precisely "the fine flavor of personality." Stickney concludes with an extended, admirably drawn portrait of Pliny as revealed in his letters, with his strengths and his weaknesses. For one not yet nineteen, this essay is remarkable in both the fluency of its language and its generous understanding. The criticism is both literary and social—and deftly aimed.

Stickney's first critical essay on poetry reviews and evaluates four volumes of poetry published within a period of two years by William Watson.[5] The essay deals with specifics but also turns to generalization often enough to give a good understanding of Stickney's views on poetry at the time. In general, these views were to be maintained, though with some important modifications, in later essays. They are based principally upon classical notions modified by the romantic concept of the great touchstone of nature. It is precisely the latter that is soon to undergo change. The poet is defined in this essay almost immediately: "I know not if an aesthete be always a poet; but a poet is certainly an aesthete, and either word, in its best sense, denotes a man who stands by the ideal, believes in it and loves it." Modern poetry suffers because idealism is not the fashion:

An honestly sad life is a lesson and a comfort for all; that despondent spirit, however, of inaction and resignation, that cheap mood, which Horace's early poems expressed once for all, is a commonplace, is poor character, and, above all, poor art. It is too often in this sense that our times are called pessimistic, it being forgotten that the disease is no new one, but has existed in all ages, though formerly it found men more ashamed of its dominance than ready for its expression.

The complaint continues that the lyric has reached an extreme of subjectivity and lacks universality:

> We are interested in ourselves, we are narrow, analytical. Our poetry is small, selfish, wholly a matter of the individual—not of the higher individual, who has something of the universal mind and, in finding expression, expresses part of that richer, vaster life, "which is the veritable history of a Human Soul," but of the lower and littler individual, the mass of freakish contradictions, whose expression cannot be edifying.

In the course of the essay Watson is criticized for specific poems that lack unity, have an excessive number of allusions, or have an appearance of refinement that has destroyed spontaneity. He is praised for his ability to capture the delicate sense of "faëry-lond" and caprice; for his ode to Autumn, which Stickney rates above Keats's, not only because it contains description but also because it is "animated with sorrow" and "musical with the grief of the bygone days"; for his sincerity; for "oddities of versification, almost Aristophanic," which "cannot but delight us after these long years of French forms and sleepy metrifying"; and because he "finds his matter close at hand in the life-issues and life-interests of the living present." Most important of all, however, he sees in Watson's poetry that "that inner communion of the poet with the transcendent life of the universe is consummated." Watson is thus "an ethical lyrist," and his poems are "ethical poems; they embody a philosophy, a teaching; they cry down an error and set forth a remedy." Stickney thus reveals the idealism and the desire for positive values that one might expect of a young man. The essay concludes with a paean to nature in the grand manner. Despite the pessimism and narrowness of the age,

> the larger freedom of the spirit remains in essence a matter of the will. And if the will be ready, where then shall we turn?

Already we stand in the diviner presences. For all true things are in Nature; and with Nature we may commune, from Nature we may learn at all times, and in Nature find our higher selves day by day.

"Herakleitos"[6] impressively demonstrates Stickney's keenness of mind in understanding Greek philosophy, and perhaps mirrors his own search for values in a world of flux. As in the majority of the essays, Germanic scholarship is condemned for its schematized approach, which results in a distorting narrowness that blinds the critic to his own subjectivity; this protest is a constant one in Stickney's critical writings. Rejecting such methods, Stickney tries to re-create something of the nature of life in ancient Ionia, the birthplace of Greek philosophy, with its marked variety of forms —in government and in topography. Herakleitos, like all early philosophers, was a physicist, and sought a physical basis for some principle that would unify the phenomena of existence in a world that seemed to be constantly changing. The answer seemed to lie in fire, water, and earth—which paradoxically could be ranked according to two contrasting scales:

> Every phaenomenon was at once retrogressive and progressive, descending and ascending, materialised and etherealised; and in the vastly elaborate physics, by which Herakleitos proved his thesis, this dual nature of the universe became the passion of life.
> Thus the restlessness of the world was at last accounted for. At the very core of life was Strife. "War," he said, "is father and king of all things."

But this is all physical, "nothing here of a distant, mystical Teutonic 'God,' who is the mentality of the world, the sum of the noumena which lie beyond our mistaken senses."

---

6. *The Harvard Monthly* 19 (February 1895) : 175–80.

Herakleitos becomes metaphysical, however, when he goes on to find fire the basic, all-pervasive element, marked by the strife of its extremes. Fire, however, is not the real absolute:

> And so Herakleitos, like all philosophers, came at last to mentality; this he said, divided itself,—implying, then, that it had a will of its own; and in the πολεμός [War, i.e., "father"] we have at last found peace,—the νόοs, δίκη, γνώμη, the ξυνόν, finally the Ζεύs, "if," he might have added, "you choose to call it so." . . . That, he says, keeps the stars musical and the worlds in their orbits; and in moments of mental calm made him use the word άρμονία —this world's harmony which springs, he says, as from a lyre or a bow.

Herakleitos thus condemned Pythagoras because "your pack of learnings teaches no νόοs," the unifying cosmic force.

Implied in this discussion is a theory of poetry of the most idealistic type imaginable (one that Stickney seemingly had from the beginning and never entirely abandoned, though the metaphysical foundations for it would seem no longer recognizable in the end). Herakleitos had found his άρμονία, the adjustment or harmony of the wold: "But in that musical chord what most struck the ear of Herakleitos was not the choral splendour of the universe; not that inspiring breath of unity which makes youth what it is and poetry possible: but rather the acid friction of overtones, that swarm of little notes which makes the best-tuned instrument sometimes painful." What the passage seems to say, among other things, is that the άρμονία is the source of the beauty of poetry. Immediately following this essay are the two poems entitled "Philosophies," in one of which man's spirit recognizes and accepts the various forms of life, all being expressions of the same power; in the other poem the point of view is that of the life force itself as it seeks newer and better forms of embodiment, culminating in intelligence.

In the essay on William Watson, Stickney implied strong approval of the poetry of Wordsworth. That poet, however, is rejected in the witty essay "Nature-Worship, Ancient and Modern. A Dialogue Between Euripides and William Wordsworth."[7] Though Wordsworth is allowed to have his say, it is obvious that he is used as a whipping boy for the repudiation of his ideas. Euripides arrives at Rydal and is amazed to find that "not a man, is there, within fifty stadia." Immediately the two clash when Wordsworth mentions the "soul," an idea Euripides finds somewhat vague. The central point of conflict, though, is nature itself. To Euripides there are two alternatives:

> That tree either contains a Dryad, or does not. If it does, then the tree, by being the home of so lovely a creature, becomes the lovelier for the almost human associations that gather round it; she has combed her long hair there, and looked at the leaves as she did so; she has been wooed by Pan, perhaps, by a Satyr, or even by a shepherd who followed her here and leaned against the huge trunk as he played on his reed. . . . Or in the other case, if there is no Dryad in the question, why, the tree is itself, green leaves, trunk and the rest of it, with no power of its own, save what you yourself choose to put into and around it.

Euripides is irritated by Wordsworth's jargon, such as "imminence [*sic*] of the Divine": "Isn't it a thing of your own, a figment of your brain, that you are projecting upon things in themselves insignificant and, as I might say, purely objective?" English literature has become superstitious, a trend intensifying under Gray and Collins and culminating in Wordsworth. The latter answers with charges of worldliness and insincerity, and talk of "the higher reaches of man and his close contact with the Infinite and Supreme." And here is the main point—Greek culture was man centered, and

7. *Ibid.* 19 (November 1894) : 62–67.

nature was judged accordingly: "to us it was the theatre for human life; the prime interest was man; a gust of passion was ever greater to us than the wind in the forest, because it was living and comprehensible." Before he is admonished to depart for London with his satchel, Wordsworth is further lectured:

> with maturity the great interest to both man and nation is life, human life. The rest amounts to very little. We know or surmise there is a divinity that shapes our ends—one of your poets won a reputation on that commonplace; but then we have our human ends to look after. Whereas you come here to the neglect of every decent human interest, and say you find everything in the contemplation of Nature. And what I mean is, it isn't there to find! No amount of reason develops a tree into a moralist, or induces you to go to school to a lake.

Of course, the cards are stacked in this game. Wordsworth loses because Stickney no longer can accept his principles. Stickney was, however, to continue writing of nature in the romantic tradition, as the really fine "Ode" of 1895 attests; nature is still worthy of our reverence, and man's finite perspective becomes lost in her eternal processes and infinite forms. But the transcendent line to a power behind Nature had been forever cut.

Several essays, all appearing in *The Harvard Monthly*, may be briefly summarized. A review of Walter Pater's *Plato and Platonism* (May 1894) finds no contribution to the study of the philosopher in the book but admits that "the form of the book grows more and more attractive, and that strange fascination of Mr. Pater's belabored style insinuates itself more deeply." Not long after the dialogue between Euripides and Wordsworth, a review of *Odes and Other Poems* appeared (January 1895). Stickney's changed position is perhaps revealed in his blanket condemnation:

> If we are to judge by this volume, Mr. Watson's technique has deteriorated with his other virtues. . . . As it is, we can but deplore that this stuff has been printed, to bring so deserving a writer into deserved disrepute.

Also rejected is Paul Elmer More's *The Great Refusal* in a review of March 1895, because "its distinctive note is pose; and in art pose is the unpardonable sin"; one learns from this essay, in a discussion of some translations, that Stickney thought highly of Leopardi's "rich sonorousness." It is perhaps an indication of his breadth of interests that Stickney bothered to write a review (May 1895) of Frank Bolles's *Chocorua's Tenants*, "ornithology in metre," which he found painful to read.

Philip Savage's *Poems* was reviewed by Stickney in June of 1895. In his friend's first volume he finds that "Nature is the pervading truth, Nature and its life by field and farm, by forest and fen." However, the spirit of Euripides is still strong in the critic:

> I confess to a feeling that the human poems are not human enough. The distress which we learn of is tainted with philosophical speculation and lacks in some degree a deeper human foundation.

Above all, most of the poems lack unity; nevertheless, there are no poses, no artificialities, and Stickney is probably as generous as he could honestly be with the volume. Horace's canon, *Aut prodesse volunt aut delectare poetae,* "poets desire either to benefit or delight"—which was changed by Renaissance critics to "teach *and* delight," is reflected in the dictum with which we are left:

> The office of poetry is, for aught that may be said to the contrary, that of teaching—teaching ways of life especially and guiding to upper places from which the prospect is large and solemn. It is a degenerate view of the art that shows us merely

pleasant colours; we are debasing it when we love it for sounds and sensations. There must be a knowledge and a truth at its heart, in order that the full gift be given.

It will not escape the reader that in essay after essay Stickney attempts to come to terms with his own art.

Something of his own developing philosophy of criticism may be seen in his review (November 1895) of R. Y. Tyrrell's *Latin Poetry*, "Lectures delivered in 1893 on the Percy Turnbull Memorial Foundation in the Johns Hopkins University." Stickney disagrees with the author's high opinion of the *Aeneid,* which he finds lacking in "sustained interest and action." Sincerity is now, as in the case of Juvenal, seen to be a difficult notion: "Indeed the greater the genius, the less does one mood exclude another, and the more violent is their juxtaposition." His summary indicates that flexibility which the comparative method of literary studies was demanding:

> If we were asked to sum up the defects of the book, we should say that Mr. Tyrrell's criticism is not dramatic, that it lacks flexibility, and displays that characteristic inability of the British mind to adjust itself to different points of view. He goes at Roman Art with something of Greek prejudice; asks of the Satire a little Greek unity; and is on the lookout for a Greek objectivity, which the Roman mind, probably less than any other, possesses. For if we are learning anything from that comparative method which the century has developed, it is that different literatures, like the peoples which produced them, cannot be judged by the same canons.

No doubt the study of Sanskrit had strengthened this position for Stickney.

From Paris Stickney sent a letter to the editors of the *Monthly* refuting criticism of *Harvard Episodes,* a book by his Cambridge classmate Charles Flandrau. The letter was published in February of 1898. Why, Stickney asks, should a work of fiction be condemned because "it does not fairly rep-

resent Harvard University"? While in Paris Stickney wrote
several reviews in French, which were translated into Italian
and published in *La Cultura*. One of these was a review of
Antonio Fogazzaro's *Il dolore nell'arte*.[8] Fogazzaro had maintained that the transitional figure—and the late nineteenth
century saw its own image as such—was a tragic one and appeared so in art. Riggs describes Stickney's objections to this
concept: "The two points which Stickney makes against
Fogazzaro may be summed up as follows: 1) the pangs of the
transitional figure are not noble and not tragic; 2) self-revela-
tion—in daylight, in full view of the public—is *bad* poetic
strategy, and an aesthetic which condones it is to be attacked."[9]
Self-pity is thus rejected as a proper attitude for the writer.
In this, as in other ways, Stickney anticipated the trend of
modern criticism.

Trumbull Stickney was one of the few to raise his voice in
defense of Edwin Arlington Robinson's *Captain Craig*, in a
review in the *Monthly* for December of 1903. Of the author
he writes that "the honesty and simplicity of his mind, the
pathos and kindness of his heart, and above all the humor
with which his imagination is lighted up continually, have
made me begin life over again and feel once more that poetry
is part of it, perhaps the truth of it." To those who complain
of the author's "plain Saxon," Stickney insists that "the test
of all forms of expression lies not in their resembling other
forms, but in their proving adequate to the thought." Concerning this review Emery Neff has written, "Stickney's
brilliantly phrased championship appeared . . . when Robinson was at the nadir of his fortunes, so fatigued that he may

---

8. *La Cultura* 19 (March 23, 1901) : 221–22.
9. Thomas Riggs, Jr., *Trumbull Stickney (1874–1904)* (Princeton dissertation, 1949) , p. 207.

not have read it for months." Neff considers Stickney's early death "a loss to criticism as well as to poetry."[10] Stickney's most extended critical writing is the longer of the two theses written for his doctorate in Paris, *Les Sentences dans La Poésie Grecque,* which was published in 1903. In the introduction Stickney puts himself somewhat in the role of what we would now call the "new critic": "Pour nous guider, il n'est qu'un seul moyen: les textes."[11] He had always disliked German criticism, and he had no patience with a methodology that tended to paralyze the critic concerned with meaning:

> Toutefois personne ne conteste que cette science, en s'attachant à des questions d'authenticité pour la plupart insolubles, a oublié que, malgré tout, le texte subsiste. . . . Nous nous y reporterons donc sans cesse; nous préférerons traduire un passage, même long et embarrassant, pourvu qu'il soit typique, plutôt que de renvoyer aux sources souvent discutables. Le texte grec, obscur, précieux ou vulgaire, logique ou incohérent, poétique, oratoire ou prosaïque, voilà non pas seulement le suject de notre étude, mais l'étude même.[12]

The *sentences* with which Stickney is concerned in this work are the *sententiae* of classical literature, the gnomic utterances or maxim-like statements which, and this is part of Stickney's theory, embody the wisdom of the tribe. His friend Henri Hubert explained this aspect of the book:

> Pour Stickney, les sentences, les *gnomai* ne sont pas l'invention d'un caprice littéraire individuel: ce sont les formes conventionnelles; transmissibles, résistantes, que prennent, pour l'usage commun, les idées générales. Elles ne naissent pas tout armées du génie d'un penseur éloquent; elles se forment au service. Elles sont sociales comme le langage.[13]

10. Emery Neff, *Edwin Arlington Robinson* (New York: William Sloane Associates, Inc., 1948) , p. 129.
11. *Les Sentences dans la Poésie Grecque,* p. 10.
12. *Ibid.,* p. 11.
13. Henri Hubert, "J. Trumbull Stickney," *Revue Archéologique,* s. 4, vol.
5 (January-June, 1905) , p. 130.

The knowledge that the *sentences* gives is like that conveyed singly in the several parts of a syllogism; it is thus a form of reasoning and can be elaborated into a full syllogism. Unlike the formulas of science, however, which are concerned with physical relations and forces, in the sentences the emphasis falls

> sur ce qui concerne les actions et sur ce que nous devons rechercher ou éviter par rapport à l'action. . . . La matière des sentences est donc générale et morale; quant à la forme, elles appartiennent à ces raisonnements par à peu près, aux termes non absolus mais probables, et qui concernent la vie, les hommes, l'action: enlevez à ces raisonnements leurs liens logiques, il reste des formules.[14]

After tracing the *sentences* through Greek literature from Homer to Euripides, Stickney arrives at some conclusions. There were two kinds of expression in Greek literature, one musical and suggestive, the other rhetorical and demonstrative. Greek literature was at its best when these two worked in harmony. However, what actually happened in the course of time was that the rhetorical element, under the influence of the orators, came to dominate: to see what a difference this made one has only to compare Sophocles with Euripides and to remember that Plato chose the dialogue rather than the drama as a form of expression. Stickney's own summary traces the decline until poets had become orators:

> Somme toute, il ressort de notre étude qu'il y a deux courants dans la poésie grecque, celui de la musique et de la pensée musicale, celui de l'éloquence et de la pensée oratoire: d'une part Pindare, de l'autre Euripide. La poésie morale se divise de même: elle est contemplative et musicale, ou elle est démonstrative et rhétorique. . . . C'est parce que la musique, qui renie le raisonnement, est venue s'associer à la poésie, que dans certains genres cette pensée abstraite s'est exprimée d'une

---

14. *Les Sentences dans la Poésie Grecque*, p. 6.

tout autre façon. Autrement dit, c'est la musique qui a fait omettre par les poètes grecs, les procédés oratoires de l'exposition abstraite. Une fois la musique passée au second plan, ils on fait des démonstrations en vers, puis eux-mêmes sont devenus des orateurs.[15]

If the musical idea seems puzzling, it should be remembered that Plato placed much importance upon music in a person's early education; to Plato it seemed to inculcate principles of order and harmony that were akin to those of mathematics, the values of which were metaphysical for the philosopher. Stickney's own explanation is directed more toward the psychology of education:

> Les Grecs . . . tout en reconnaissant l'effet de la musique sur les sens, savaient fort bien que, elle aussi, elle se rattache à des facultés intellectuelles. . . . La musique, qui évoque les sentiments profonds et secrets, les a comme suscités en eux. Absente, ils ont fait des théorèmes en vers.

Logic and music blend together then into a harmonious whole:

> Ce rapport est des plus naturels. Qu'on imagine un esprit pour lequel, d'une part, la musique est trop hors de la logique, trop vague, trop sensuelle et, en prenant ce mot au sens propre, trop peu intelligible; pour lequel, d'autre part, la démonstration oratoire ou philosophique est trop sèche, trop artificielle et, dans cette mesure fausse.[16]

Perhaps one can add to this that music not only aids the memory, but it also works on the emotions of men, which have to be receptive to logic if true learning is to take place; such, at any rate, would seem to be Stickney's meaning here, in a passage that reminds us that the ancient writers were making a complex appeal to man's mind and heart.

---

15. *Ibid.*, p. 253.
16. *Ibid.*, pp. 254–55.

Judging from what he had accomplished by the time of his death, we may say that had Stickney lived he might have become a really first-rate critic. Certainly he was well prepared for the job of criticism. His classical studies had developed firmly within him a desire for a literature that would be, not in the modern derogatory sense, but in the classical sense, didactic—concerned with the important issues of man's existence in his daily relationship with other men, with nature as his theatre of life, and with the metaphysical questions relating to his overall destiny. He had also mastered the comparative method, which demanded that a critic judge a work of literature on its own merit and in terms of the culture that produced it before comparing it with the literature of another country (Stickney discusses *sentences* in Sanskrit and how they differ from those in Greek in one section of his thesis). It is surely no exaggeration to say that he possessed one of the best-trained minds in America at the time of his death. One must remember the cosmopolitan quality of this mind when he reads the poetry of Trumbull Stickney.

4

Stickney and the Critics

Copies of *The Poems of Trumbull Stickney,* which appeared in 1905, have now become quite rare. Stickney's reputation as a poet was kept alive by anthologies edited by such prominent figures as Conrad Aiken, William Rose Benét, David Cecil, Allen Tate, F. O. Matthiessen, Louis Untermeyer, Mark Van Doren, W. H. Auden, and Oscar Williams.[1] The editors of one of the most recent anthologies to include Stickney consider him "the most conspicuously neglected of all American poets."[2] Despite the service they have rendered to Stickney's reputation, anthologists are often influenced by each other and by the length of a poem; for Stickney it is unfortunately true that many of the poems frequently anthologized are inferior to a number of others in the *Poems.* Of the anthologists, Conrad Aiken has included

1. A helpful but not entirely accurate aid is J. Wm. Meyers, "A Complete Stickney Bibliography," *Twentieth Century Literature* 9 (January 1964) : 209–12. See also *Bulletin of Bibliography and Magazine Notes* 26 (July–Sept. 1969) : 83–85.

2. *A New Canon of English Poetry,* ed. James Reeves and Martin Seymour-Smith (London: Heinemann Educational Books, Ltd., 1967) , p. xvii.

Stickney in three collections, referring to him in one as "the natural link between Dickinson and the twentieth-century 'thing.' "[3] *Homage to Trumbull Stickney,* a small volume of poems selected by James Reeves and Seán Haldane, was published by Heinemann in 1968; it contains a rather polemical introduction and review of criticism, which emphasizes Stickney's "intensity" and condemns critics for failing to see his greatness as a poet. Haldane has also written *The Fright of Time: Joseph Trumbull Stickney 1874–1904* (Ladysmith, Quebec: Ladysmith Press, 1970), a conjectural biography based primarily upon Stickney's letters to his sister Lucy.

Not a great many critics have commented upon Stickney, but those who have taken the trouble to examine his work have had some interesting things to say about it. Perhaps the first significant critic was his close friend William Vaughn Moody. Moody was blind to some of Stickney's faults because he was speaking of a friend and because they were, to a large extent, his own faults as well. Nevertheless, he was certainly correct in noticing "the emotion of homelessness, which runs in a haunting undertone through his poems" and in saying that Stickney "dreamed of making in his own poetry I know not what new synthesis of Eastern with Western thought."[4]

In 1933 R. P. Blackmur reviewed Stickney's poetry and concentrated upon its weaknesses:

> He hovered—not only in the last year of his life, but always in the twelve years of writing of which we have record—constantly on the perilous balance where it is determined whether a man write sound verse or dilute his emotions in words. . . . He simply had not reached the point where, no longer a pour-

3. Conrad Aiken, ed., *Twentieth-Century American Poetry* (New York: Random House, Inc., 1944), p. xxii.
4. William Vaughn Moody, "The Poems of Trumbull Stickney," *The North American Review* 183 (November 16, 1906): 1007.

ing-out into existing greedy form, poetry becomes, with some sacrifice of self-expression, a difficult objective art.[5]

To Blackmur, Stickney is a poet of lines and phrases.

The most important critic of Stickney's work has been Edmund Wilson, who dismisses the monologues and dramas as unsuccessful but admits that "there is a real poet in Stickney."[6] After quoting "Mnemosyne" he calls attention to the simple but effective images in the poem which remind him of Pushkin and Robert Frost:

> This spareness and simplicity of language that carries a charge of meaning is quite unlike the decadent romanticism that reigned at the end of the century. . . . It was what Trumbull Stickney had that was really impressive and original. You find it often in the last line of his poems.[7]

With penetrating insight Wilson continues by calling attention to a basic conflict in Stickney's verse:

> What is behind the best poetry of Stickney is a conflict between the desired and the possible much more serious than the wistfulness of the nineties. It is evidently one of those New England conflicts such as we get in the heroes of Henry James: the struggle of the desire to live against cramped habits and a dead tradition. . . . And thus the most effective images of Stickney—the soldered eyelids, the slanted door, the girl who closes her window, the desolated country of childhood—all represent the poet as shut out from some source of beauty or life. Trumbull Stickney's real strength lies in his not being content to pretend, as other poets of the period did . . . that the putting-on of exotic costumes gives one the right to speak in the name of the feelings of their original wearers. Stickney is enough of a poet on occasion to throw off the costume and speak for himself.[8]

5. R. P. Blackmur, "Stickney's Poetry," *Poetry: A Magazine of Verse* 42 (June 1933) : 159–60.
6. Edmund Wilson, "The Country I Remember," *The New Republic* 103 (October 14, 1940) : 529.
7. *Ibid.,* p. 530.
8. *Ibid.* As late as 1966 Wilson listed Stickney and Robinson as writers of first-rate poetry in America between the time of Poe and that of Pound. See *Patriotic Gore* (New York: Oxford University Press, 1966) , p. 503.

In their *A History of American Poetry, 1900–1940,* Horace Gregory and Marya Zaturenska assert that while reading Stickney "one seems to stand in the unshaded presence of poetic genius."[9] The impression is only a temporary one, however, as faults soon begin to appear. The authors point out that "individual lines and stanzas revive a personality precociously gifted in its sensibility to an elegiac note in poetry (which is a classical heritage that British and American literature has carried from the past into our own day) ."[10] Emery Neff goes even further and calls Stickney "the only American poet at the turn of the century besides Robinson, Frost, and Santayana to have achieved an individual style."[11] This brief survey of critical estimates may be concluded with Louise Bogan's observation that "Stickney broke with no traditions; but his quality is impressively pure, and, both as a man and an artist, he is the one American of his day who belongs to the world of finely tempered human beings with which, in the same period, Henry James in his last great phase was occupying himself."[12]

Because of the loss of most of Stickney's letters to his friends, it is rather difficult to know beyond doubt what he read that might have influenced his own poetry. Critics have been in general agreement about the matter, however. As early as 1898, in a letter to Robert Morss Lovett, Moody, who should have known, wrote of "the synthesis of Browning with Verlaine, at which he manifestly aims."[13] René Taupin also saw Browning and Verlaine as influences ("In Summer"

9. *A History of American Poetry, 1900–1940* (New York: Harcourt, Brace and Company, 1946) , p. 33.

10. *Ibid.,* p. 36.

11. *Edwin Arlington Robinson* (New York: William Sloane Associates, Inc., 1948) , p. 129.

12. *Achievement in American Poetry, 1900–1950* (Chicago: Henry Regnery Company, 1951) , p. 32.

13. *Some Letters of William Vaughn Moody,* ed. Daniel Gregory Mason (Boston and New York: Houghton Mifflin Company, 1913) , p. 97.

being an example of the influence of the latter) but went on to say: "dans ces vers Stickney n'imite que Verlaine, mais son désir le plus fervent fut de réaliser une poésie où l'influence de Tennyson tempérerait celle de Verlaine."[14] Wilson also saw the influence of Verlaine in a poem such as "Mnemosyne" but argues that "it has in it something stronger and more masculine than '*Il pleut dans mon coeur*' and the rest."[15]

A point added by Horace Gregory and Marya Zaturenska is of perhaps more significance than has been recognized: "If one looks for literary influence in its best sense, it would seem that Stickney read Keats and John Webster with more understanding and intelligence than his contemporaries." The last fragment in the *Poems* is said to have "a touch of Webster's violence."[16]

Larzer Ziff makes the interesting comment that Stickney "could not turn to the anti-poetic of Whitman, because this indeed was linked in his mind with the science and commerce which had smashed values. As a result he remained trapped within the house of tradition, searching for some way to make its furniture function for modern use."[17] Ziff's criticism is somewhat misleading. It is true for a good many of Stickney's poems; but, as the different influences noted by critics suggest, Stickney actually has a number of styles, depending upon the kind of poem he was writing. One can best understand his style by examining these types and specific poems within them.

14. René Taupin, *L'Influence du Symbolisme Français sur La Poésie Américaine (De 1910 A 1920)* (Paris: Librairie Ancienne Honoré Champion, 1929), pp. 54, 62.
15. P. 530.
16. P. 35.
17. *The American 1890s* (New York: The Viking Press, 1966), p. 314.

5

The Dramatic Mode

Throughout his life Trumbull Stickney had a pronounced
interest in drama. In his undergraduate days at Harvard he
participated as an actor in plays given in various languages.
The title of the only volume of verse that he himself saw
through the press was, after all, *Dramatic Verses;* and, after
his stay in Paris, upon his return to Harvard for the year
1903–04 he was instrumental in developing plans for the
production of a Greek play, the *Choephoroe* of Aeschylus,
which was to be presented by the Department of Classics the
next year.[1] His early death prevented him from taking the
lead in this play.

That Stickney's interest in the dramatic mode was persistent is indicated by a note in the 1905 edition of his
Poems: "At the time of his death Stickney was contemplating
the publication of a volume to be called 'Dramatic Scenes'.
. . ."[2] The work dealing with the young manhood of Ben-

1. E. K. Rand, "Joseph Trumbull Stickney," *The Harvard Graduates'
Magazine* 13 (December 1904) : 243.
2. *The Poems of Trumbull Stickney* (Boston and New York: Houghton
Mifflin & Co., 1905) , p. 215.

venuto Cellini was to have been included in this volume. It was William Vaughn Moody's opinion that "Stickney's lyric work may be said, speaking fallibly, to be complete. If he had lived he would have added to it much that was precious, but he would perhaps not have surpassed his present achievement in kind. His career as a dramatic poet was, on the other hand, assuredly only begun."[3] Moody's estimation is partly a reflection of his own career and interests, but it would seem to express accurately enough Stickney's own interest as well. Stickney was working almost concurrently upon dramatic poems that fall into two categories, dramatic monologues and dramatic scenes.

i. Dramatic Monologues

The earliest and most original of the dramatic monologues is "Oneiropolos" (1897). The poem contrasts the meditative, spiritual quality of life in ancient India with the obsession with action and the materialistic that has characterized the West, represented by Athens in the poem. Oneiropolos (the name the speaker has taken, if it was not his original name), caught up in the movement of people caused by the conquests of Alexander, has come to Athens and makes his living telling fortunes, "selling to Athens dreams." The Athenians worship the glory they had achieved during the height of the classical period, but they are now a declining race, spiritually devoid of qualities necessary for greatness.

The light imagery of the poem is perhaps a reflection of the Buddha's Fire Sermon, for as it is used in reference to Athens it suggests a decadence and spiritual restlessness: "burned by sunlight thro' the stifling hours,/ Temple and

---

3. "The Poems of Trumbull Stickney," *The North American Review* 183 (November 16, 1906) : 1012.

house, statue and wall and road/ Glow as hot copper."
Oneiropolos thinks of his guru Brihadashua, who taught him
self-conquest and the mastery of desire:

> To him, as one who rushes head aflame,
> Kindled and dry with fever, toward shore,
> I went; and most divinely pitiful
> He taught me wisdom. . . .

The Athenians are "this Grecian race of laughter, pleasure,
song" and lack "anything/ That makes the spirit pure."
Even their philosophers are "drunken and sense-tied to the
trembling world." The only person in Athens who has values
similar to those of Oneiropolos is Epicurus, who aids the poor
and teaches them wisdom, "for many hear/ The spoken
solace of his quietude." The diction of "Oneiropolos" is itself
tempered by the spirit of India:

>   I quit the shore
> Of holy Ganga's healing water-wave,
> Long travelled, breathed of many airs, reviewed
> Forests of sandal, where the Spring wind blew,
> And tender-petalled lily-beds, whereo'er
> The gray crane spanned his gracious, level flight.

The other dramatic monologues are strongly influenced
by Robert Browning, in regard to both theme and diction.
"Lodovico Martelli" (1898) centers on the dying hours of
a minor poet who has "nothing timeless said!" Martelli has
not even lived long enough to write the poems he has *felt*,
and the poem emphasizes the fact that his perceptions of life
are highly poetic. Martelli tells of a fight he had with a
masked figure over a courtesan. The masked figure proves to
be Pope Leo! Now Martelli is probably being poisoned in
Sicily, while his memory constantly returns to his native

Firenze; he is thus a character in exile, a recurrent motif in
Stickney's poetry. Like the remaining dramatic monologues
to be discussed, "Lodovico Martelli" is so strongly indebted
to Browning that the reader can never forget Browning.
There are, nevertheless, some striking images in the poem,
as in the passage that describes the seductive courtesan who
"laughs like beech-leaves ringing in the light," or the one
that begins with an echo from Homer but becomes something new while portraying the change from day to night:

> And far abroad
> From Even's distaff floats the purple wool.
> Wet-eyed she sits; the light for love of her
> Becomes a moon but to behold her die—

"Requiescam" (1900) is based upon the notion that an
artist skillful in one medium always desires to try another
one. The idea is of course made quite clear in Browning's
"One Word More," and Stickney uses it in the second "In
Ampezzo" poem, where the desire is for a combination of
the arts to capture a vision of nature. The persona of
"Requiescam" is a sculptor who decides that "landscape will
ease me somewhat toward the end." This hope is revealed
to a painter, and in the first version of the poem there was a
poet also. The long struggle of the artist to capture an ideal
is directly related to the evolutionary process:

> In a bole of clay all my life long
> I've stared my visions in, and, thumbing, seen
> Materialize obscurely to a line
> The long desire of Nature turning home.
> So strains itself out of the sea a shape
> With loads of weedy tide up to the land,
> Straining fore'er miserably unsatisfied.

This struggle can lead at the extreme only to great disappoint-

ment, "for by our bases we're firm sunken-down/ In the element." "Requiescam" reminds one of an earlier untitled
monologue, "Hold still, my brain! My temples burst!" (1895–
96). In this poem a sculptor is working on a marble from
Paros, "an isle/ [That] Does make earth more magnificent
than aught/ Of conquest." From the marble the sculptor
would create an Aphrodite:

> She shall be here eternally while I
> Make her eternal. I shall bid her come,
> Sit near, and say things in her golden Greek,
> And singing freshen some old mythos with
> Warm melody. . . .

Of Stickney's dramatic monologues only "Oneiropolos"
contains enough originality of conception and language to
make it appealing. Stickney's study of Sanskrit literature is
reflected in the poem; this interest in Indian thought is revealed in other poems as well, and the contrast between East
and West that lies at the heart of "Oneiropolos" is a theme
that was to be used later by T. S. Eliot. All the other monologues are so strongly in the tradition of Browning and so
heavily indebted to him that they can scarcely impress a
modern reader.

ii. Dramatic Scenes

Stickney's dramatic scenes are more interesting than the
monologues, although half of them are unfinished, a fact
which may suggest some apprehension on the part of the
author as to his success in the dramatic mode. Despite his
consistent interest in drama and the dramatic in poetry,
Stickney is original as a poet only in the lyric mode. The
fragment of "The Cardinal Play" (1897), which Moody

thought so important (of the editors of the *Poems* it was probably Moody who so described it) ,[4] Stickney evidently abandoned as having little promise. The fragment is so short that it is difficult to judge, but its theme of incest and the Renaissance posturing of the characters suggest an initial bad start. The fragment opens with a Cardinal ordering his son to seek out the person who abducted the daughter of a jeweler who has done some work for the Cardinal. The son is shocked at this request from a father he knows to be lacking in piety but slowly comes to realize that the jeweler's daughter is in actuality the daughter of the Cardinal and, therefore, his own sister. Of course it is the Cardinal's son who has fled with the girl and who is now shocked at the incest he has committed. Only Moody's enthusiasm for drama could have seen in this situation something worth further development. The debt to Browning is perhaps again obvious in the view of the powerful but corrupt clergy of the Renaissance.

In July of 1902 when Moody went to Paris to visit Stickney for a month, the two read the entire Greek tragedy together. Stickney had already written *Prometheus Pyrphoros* (1900) , a dramatic scene of almost seven hundred lines. Stickney's influence upon Moody was an important one, as a Moody scholar has stated: "for his later and deeper interest in Greek literature he was largely indebted to Trumbull Stickney, whose influence upon him Moody rated high."[5] Moody himself was to deal with the Prometheus theme, most explicitly in *The Fire-Bringer* of 1904. Stickney's close friend George Cabot Lodge treated similar material in his *Cain* (1904) and *Herakles* (1908) .

---

4. *Poems*, p. 285.
5. *The Poems and Plays of William Vaughn Moody*, with an Introduction by John M. Manly (Boston and New York: Houghton Mifflin Company, 1912) , 1:xxxi.

Moody added a note to the 1905 edition of Stickney's *Poems* in which he pointed out that Stickney had dealt with the Prometheus theme before he himself had. He also stated that "those who are curious to examine the sources of the *Prometheus Pyrphoros* will find them in the account given by Hesiod, supplemented in some details by that of the mythographer Apollodorus."[6] There is no similarity between Stickney's work and that of Shelley in *Prometheus Unbound*.

Prometheus Pyrphoros opens with "total obscurity, nothing on the scene being distinguishable." This situation has come about because Prometheus has tricked Zeus with an offering judged to be an insult. As a punishment Zeus has withdrawn all fire and light. The reactions of the various characters to this initial situation represent the differing attitudes men seem to have in the face of the tragedy of life itself. Epimetheus, Prometheus's brother, is obsessed by the past:

> No daylight.
> Nor anything on before; but at my back
> Remembrance made a weary song, chanting
> The mellow seasons that have gone away.

His son, Deukalion, is angered by the regret of his father and by the eternal hope of Prometheus:

> Aye, 't is we suffer their temerities,
> And back and forth, to ends we know not of,
> Madden between to-morrow and yesterday.

Only Deukalion's wife, Pyrrha, expresses confidence in Prometheus's ability to remedy the situation.

Prometheus's outlook on life is entirely man centered: "We

---

6. *Poems*, p. 105.

are the crown of nature and her lord." Such salvation as is
possible will be achieved only by human hands:

> We change and pass away,
> But so in changing have some mastery, we
> Revolving make progression, we endure
> In virtue of desire and hope dissatisfied,
> And, thro' disaster struggling, at the last
> Fetch in salvation and the human end.

With this end in view he departs to steal back the fire from
heaven. Deukalion predicts what the result will be, from, of
course, his own point of view:

> He will hang out in anguish crucified
> Upon the giddy ramparts of the world
> While we mysteriously damned shall hide
> Here at night's bottom to the last of time.

Prometheus's success is indicated by the light that covers
the scene before his return. Once back he tells of his struggle
up to heaven in a long passage in which Stickney uses an
imaginary landscape for Prometheus's journey; the vast distance and the ordeal of Prometheus are both made vivid
through this description, for which Stickney was probably
indebted to the notion that Mount Olympus was originally
the home of the Greek gods. Prometheus's victory is one that
cannot be erased, no matter what punishment might be
meted out to him:

> I say, whate'er's achieved, once and for all
> Stands in defiance, and we at Nature's heart
> Register signs of our nobility.
> This is the symbol I have had my will,
> Which down the crystal stairs into the depth
> I bore, a little flame thro' darkness, won
> From summits which henceforth are counted ours.
> With it I've lit the world. . . .

For this accomplishment he must, of course, pay the inevitable price; and at the end of the drama he is led away by the
Voices of Zeus. Pyrrha reflects that "to-morrow brings again/
The sun he gave us, and the hope—the life." With these
words the poem ends.

There is another character in *Prometheus Pyrphoros,* one
whose role is difficult to determine. Pandora is never seen;
only her voice is heard in song, and it is "always as from
within." She has become pregnant by Zeus, and as a result, as
Pyrrha realizes, is in the possession of knowledge not shared
by other mortals. At intervals throughout the play she sings,
and her first song reflects her more than human awareness:

> *The lips of Gods and mortals in a dream*
> *Have lain on my lips of a summer night:*
> *They fade like images down-stream,*
> *But I have remained behind the light.*

Riggs is no doubt correct in suggesting that "she represents
some kind of a feminine principle in nature: gross matter
impregnated by divinity. . . . But in the process she has as-
sumed a more primitive reality than that of her impregnator,
and both Gods and mortals fade away while she remains."[7]
In yet another song her distance from the human scene is
emphasized:

> *Before my eyes they come and go;*
> *The shadows on my dreaming face*
> *Move to and fro,*
> *Yet I look further over larger ways.*
> *For pity is not of that nor this,*
> *And kindness stretches out her arm*
> *On all that is,*
> *To keep the grass-blade and the star from harm.*

---

7. Thomas Riggs, Jr., "Prometheus 1900," *American Literature* 22 (January 1951) : 410.

One is reminded of Moody's statement that Stickney "dreamed of making in his own poetry I know not what new synthesis of Eastern with Western thought."[8]

It is probably the tension created by the different views of Pandora and of Prometheus in the play that has caused two critics to see Stickney's Prometheus drama as a failure. Ziff comments that "Prometheus, when he brings light, does so like a magnanimous being acting in the face of a hopeless situation, but the specific gift holds out little realizable promise for humanity."[9] Such a statement ignores the symbolic value of the deed. Prometheus's victory is one of the spirit and can exist only on an individual basis; therefore, it cannot be transferred to others, beyond providing an example. More devastating is the criticism of Thomas Riggs, Jr., who compares Stickney's treatment of Prometheus and the idea of progress with the work of Moody and Lodge, as well as that of their elder friend, Henry Adams. However, Stickney's poem is perhaps not so sharply focused on the idea of progress as Riggs's comparison implies. Seeing the matter as he does, Riggs concludes that "the action of the poem is conceived as an assertion, however bleak, of progress, but the emotional weight is on the side of the laws of dissipation [of energy] and decay. In Stickney's case the matter has not yet become fully available to the mind, but is felt darkly."[10]

Moody himself was nearer the truth when he argued that "the triumph [of Prometheus] lies in the deed itself and in the magnanimity which achieved it. It is very characteristic of Stickney's line of thought that he should have given this turn to the great story." Moody continues by discussing

---

8. "The Poems of Trumbull Stickney," p. 1007.
9. Larzar Ziff, *The American 1890s, Life and Times of a Lost Generation* (New York: The Viking Press, 1966), p. 315.
10. Riggs, "Prometheus 1900," p. 409.

Stickney's personal "sense of the futility of the worldly out-
come," mentioned earlier in the first chapter of this study,
and goes ahead to maintain that for Stickney "the important
thing was seen to be, not the nature of our destiny, but the
manner in which it is met."[11] Moody knew Stickney well
enough to be aware of his attitude toward this subject, and
his interpretation is supported by a number of other poems
by Stickney, such as the "Fragment of an Ode for Greek
Liberty," which asserts that "it needs not to have won/ To
be great." There is nobility in man's struggle, even though
he be defeated, so long as there "stands forth our Nikè, proud,
tho' broken-winged" ("Tho' lack of laurels and of wreaths
not one"). Actually, the fragment called "The Soul of Time,"
which Riggs quotes as resolving the philosophic difficulties of
Prometheus Pyrphoros, will support the interpretation given
here, since it offers two views of time, one from the perspective of eternity and the other from man's own limited point
of view. Because man's view is thus limited, it does not follow
that his actions are without merit. Prometheus's struggle is
in some ways like that of Camus's Sisyphus, who strives without ceasing to assert his human dignity in a world devoid
of other values.

Perhaps the most ambitious undertaking on Stickney's
part in the dramatic mode was his plan for writing an extended drama dealing with the life of Julian the Apostate.
Of this nothing remains except a fragment of a work begun
in 1901. The *Poems* contains a brief note on the fragment,
but Moody is more explicit about Stickney's plans in his
article:

> It is a thousand pities that he was not able to finish the Julian.
> There was much in his own character and training to give him
> peculiar insight into the mind of the poet, scholar, satirist,

---

11. "The Poems of Trumbull Stickney," p. 1018.

soldier and world-ruler who, at the moment when pagan
civilization was about to be overwhelmed forever by the mount-
ing tide of Christian thought, arose to declare again the
ancient gods and to rekindle with indignant hands the violated
altars. Stickney intended to write a two-act play in the nature
of a prelude, treating the life of Julian before his elevation to
the throne, and a five-act drama dealing with his career as
emperor.[12]

Exactly what Stickney might have done with this idea is difficult to tell, but it is clear that the play would have portrayed
Julian as essentially a noble figure trying to save the classical
culture that was being displaced or absorbed by Christianity.
The fragment begins with the period when Gallus, who had
been made Caesar and appointed to rule at Antioch, has
been overthrown by the suspicious Constance (Constantius
II), who then summons Gallus's half-brother Julian to court
to examine him in terms of his own ambitions and in regard
to his supposed paganism.

The scene opens amid the intrigue of the Christian court,
where the most heinous crimes committed by the state are
rationalized in Machiavellian fashion, religion being used
hypocritically to mask these deeds. Before Julian's arrival a
messenger enters and relates the story of the putting to death
of Gallus upon the orders of Constance. Shortly after Julian
enters he learns what has happened and fears that he too is
to be killed. In contrast to the other characters, Julian appears
to be essentially a scholar, uninterested in wielding worldly
power:

My study long has lain
In things forgot, or nearly; and of them
The shadows lengthening at later day
And spiritual out of the sun's great heart
In violet, in crimson, and in gold

12. *Ibid.*, p. 1013.

> Walk the forlorn campanias, to the sound
> Of Homer's hymns in order filing on
> Between Ionian columns—

and when questioned further concerning his associates, his
answer is filled with irony, as he asserts that they are

> Merely philosophers and pagan priests,
> Who in the brain's high nonsense are embarked
> On seas of error, wastes of speculation,
> After the quest and mirage of the truth.
> Pity for them, my Lords! Had they been able,
> They'd vowed their vulgar lives to better ends,
> To court and office, manners, money, and
> The brilliant business of ambition;
> Also, they'd long abandoned the ancient creed,
> Abandoned long ago beliefs that—they'd
> Been converts to the new, but that their souls,
> Saturate and all kneaded up in one
> With dull ideals of an extinguished world,
> Live in them and go like drunken mariners
> Bows-on for folly and th' enormous night.

Eusebia, the Queen, who has taken a rather motherly interest
in Julian, talks the King into merely keeping the young man
under observation. This is all that remains of the play, except
for a few brief fragments of Act II. The Julian piece is indebted to Renaissance drama in its emphasis on court intrigue and in its very language, a good example being this
conceit in which the King reveals his fear of treachery:

> Around my throne I feel a sea of snakes
> Rocking their heads, and struck I each new day
> A score of them, the tide still hisses in
> Snapping its poisoned whips. To keep alive
> And steer this kingdom forward into time,
> It needs a thousand eyes, and in the skull
> Brains like an ant-hill.

There are other, more original passages of interest, such as the one that describes a man suddenly awakened who has reason to fear for his life: " 'Quick up!'/ Barbatio said to the man, and in his eyes/ Two sparks grew big and died." Also of interest is the fine passage from a fragment of Act II which begins with "The rarer gift/ Is in the uses of imagination"; the lines that follow deal with the difficulty of expressing a felt ideal or of maintaining it in the world of everyday reality, and with the tragedy that is often the result of this ironic situation: "as if/ Genius were a debt of Man to Nature/ Paid alive on itself."

Stickney's last dramatic scene was begun in 1903 and completed on January 28, 1904, the year of his death. It is concerned with the young manhood of Benvenuto Cellini, the great Italian metalsmith and sculptor, whose turbulent, often violent life is related in his *Autobiography*. Benvenuto is apprenticed to a goldsmith against the wishes of his father, who desires him to be a musician. The young man's admiration for Michelangelo causes him to become involved in a fight when the great artist is insulted. After another conflict with his father, Benvenuto decides to run away to Rome in pursuit of his art.

It is worthy of notice that the best part of this dramatic scene is a song containing the following lines:

> *I waited for her near her farm*
> *Close up beside a cypress tree.*
> *The road lay white as linen by,*
> *And moonlight made the meadow warm.*

This is indicative of the fact that Trumbull Stickney's true gift as a poet, despite his long and persistent interest in drama, was in the lyric mode. His finest achievement in the dramatic mode is the *Prometheus* piece, which puts him in a tradition that began in the late nineteenth century in America, when poets such as Hovey, Moody, and Robinson were led to use medieval and classical myths as ways of structuring contemporary themes. All of these poets tried to master verse drama, for which they had the highest regard as a literary form. As Malcolm Cowley has observed,[13] the natural heir of this tradition was another Harvard product, T. S. Eliot, who combined a deep interest in classical literature with a desire to use it to express the predicament of modern man and who labored long to master verse drama himself.

---

13. *The Literary Situation* (New York: The Viking Press, 1954) , p. 244.

6

The Landscape of the Mind

Trumbull Stickney's poetry abounds with landscape imagery, of which there are two distinct kinds. The first type of imagery serves as the skeleton of the poem; that is, landscape is used as the basic metaphor of the poem, uniting it in terms of focus and evocation. There are probably less than half a dozen of Stickney's poems which are so constructed; but at least two of them—the first one of two bearing the title "In Ampezzo," and "Mnemosyne"—are among his finest achievements, and several of the others are quite remarkable in some respects.

The second type of landscape imagery to be found in Stickney's poetry is more abundant and is used generally within the scope of a few lines as a metaphor or symbol but does not dominate the entire poem, as in the case of the first type. This second type will be called "the Landscape of the Mind," because when it is employed the poet objectifies inner emotions and attitudes through the use of landscape imagery. It is this kind of imagery which is unique in Stickney's poetry, and it is of such a complexity that it may be broken down into several categories for the purposes of analysis. It is helpful, however, to begin by examining the first kind of landscape imagery in order to determine what qualities it possesses. It will be obvious to the reader that the two types are in reality related, since the first type also reflects the inner feeling of the persona of the poem. The *essential* difference lies in the relationship of the imagery to the poem as a whole.

i. Landscape Poems

It was Edmund Wilson who first commented on Stickney's use of landscape as a controlling metaphor: "In a poem like the first piece called 'In Ampezzo' in the volume of collected poems, the resisting integument has been broken by an expansion of sensibility that meets, merges into, possesses, some landscape with its atmosphere of a moment."[1] In his unpublished dissertation on Stickney, Thomas Riggs, Jr., called this kind of poem "the landscape with figure, which he had developed from Lamartine and de Musset and refined for his own purposes."[2] Actually, landscape has been used for a long time in poetry. Certainly the Greek and Roman classics make considerable use of landscape, especially in the genre usually termed *pastoral*. The pastoral elegy in particular has employed landscape in order to reflect the varying moods of the poet; this has been true from the time of Theocritus and his classical imitators to that of Milton, Shelley, and Arnold, all of whom wrote elegies in the classical tradition. Other kinds of poems have employed landscape as a central metaphor reflecting a complex state of mind or awareness, Pope's

1. Edmund Wilson, " 'The Country I Remember,' " *The New Republic* 103 (October 14, 1940) : 529.
2. Thomas Riggs, Jr., *Trumbull Stickney (1874–1904)* (Princeton dissertation, 1949) , p. 216.

"Windsor Forest" being a notable example. The Romantics
also produced poems dependent upon landscape for their
structural unity, Wordsworth's "Tintern Abbey" being perhaps the best known. There is, therefore, a long tradition for
the use of landscape in poetry, and it is no doubt impossible
to point accurately to one poet or period as Stickney's source.
"Mnemosyne" will serve as a good example of the kind of
poem being considered here. It is, despite several weaknesses,
a fine poem and is worthy of being quoted in its entirety:

It's autumn in the country I remember.

How warm a wind blew here about the ways!
And shadows on the hillside lay to slumber
During the long sun-sweetened summer-days.

It's cold abroad the country I remember.

The swallows veering skimmed the golden grain
At midday with a wing aslant and limber;
And yellow cattle browsed upon the plain.

It's empty down the country I remember.

I had a sister lovely in my sight:
Her hair was dark, her eyes were very sombre;
We sang together in the woods at night.

It's lonely in the country I remember.

The babble of our children fills my ears,
And on our hearth I stare the perished ember
To flames that show all starry thro' my tears.

It's dark about the country I remember.

There are the mountains where I lived. The path

Is slushed with cattle-tracks and fallen timber,
The stumps are twisted by the tempests' wrath.

But that I knew these places are my own,
I'd ask how came such wretchedness to cumber
The earth, and I to people it alone.

It rains across the country I remember.

Here the kaleidoscope of memory plays upon the conscious-ness, which interprets the scenes by means of the refrain. The lovely lyricism of the poem stems from Stickney's skill-ful variations upon "the country I remember" line and is reinforced by the sharp visual details. Careful reading of the poem further reveals a content that is surprising in its com-plexity and in its strikingly modern philosophy. Although the poem is undated, 1901 would be a reasonable guess as to the time of composition, because the poem is obviously not an early production and was included in *Dramatic Verses* of 1902. The persona of the poem is carried back to different periods of the past, and his attitude toward the experiences is reflected in the varying refrain. The poem moves from a child's sensuous perception of summer, to a youth's visual awareness of living nature, to an adolescent's need for com-panionship, to the responsibility of parenthood, to the lone-liness of old age. While the fourth stanza may seem exces-sively sentimental, it might be defended in terms of the total philosophy of the poem, for it is often the responsibilities of adulthood that make a man most aware of his limitations, of the fact that certain dreams are gone forever.

"Mnemosyne" is in a sense a poem about the disintegra-tion of dreams. In the last two stanzas, which are emphasized by the fact that they deal with one period, the *present*, with no intervening refrain, the persona contemplates in amazement what has happened to his life. The imagery of these two stanzas admirably conveys the sense of isolation and of desolation which the persona feels so strongly, the loneliness being suggested with singular force by the use of "to people" as a verb. Put in other words, "Mnemosyne" is about the disintegration of the concept of *self*, for as the speaker looks back over his life he finds little if any continuity between the past and the present; indeed, the contrast between the past and present results in shock for the speaker himself. One is reminded of Samuel Beckett's somewhat similar theme in *Krapp's Last Tape*.[3]

"At Sainte-Marguerite" (1902?) is in some ways a perplexing poem. It may be indebted to Arnold's *Switzerland*, with its theme of isolation, and to his "The Buried Life," which deals with the difficulties of communicating one's deepest emotions and desires even when one is aware of them. Stickney's poem would seem to center upon the moment of awareness. The scene is set in the opening stanza:

> The gray tide flows and flounders in the rocks
> Along the crannies up the swollen sand.
> Far out the reefs lie naked—dunes and blocks
> Low in the watery wind. A shaft of land
> Going to sea thins out the western strand.

The second stanza opens with two lines that illustrate Stickney's ability to sometimes capture details in a unique manner: "It rains, and all along and always gulls/ Career seascreaming in and weather-glossed." It is not only time for the tide; it is also the time for the subtle change of season. The speaker has come to this place of "desolation" while "Inland a little way the summer lies," with "the harvest's

---

3. See Martin Esslin's discussion in *The Theatre of the Absurd* (Garden City, N. Y.: Doubleday & Company, Inc., 1961), pp. 41–42.

mellow residue." This contrast between scenes at the period of seasonal change is a recurring motif in Stickney's poetry. Into this coastal setting the persona has come for reasons uncertain to himself:

> Was it to pluck this savage from the schist,
> This crazy yellowish bloom without a name,
> With leathern blade and tortured wiry frame?

In other words, to find a remnant of beauty amid a scene of desolation, another recurring motif. The heart of the poem, however, is concerned with the relationship between the persona and the sea, for there is a desire for a kind of purging like that which the sea may be imagined to provide for the land:

> to let go
> Down the ravine one with another, down
> Across the surf to linger or to drown
>
> The loves that none can give and none receive,
> The fearful asking and the small retort,
> The life to dream of and the dream to live!

This act of purgation the sea can perform for itself: "Thou art thy Priest, thy Victim and thy God."

One of the "Sonnets From Greece," "Mt. Lykaion," (1903), dramatically illustrates the relationship between the poet and the landscape he contemplates and concerns a theme not found in any of the other landscape poems under discussion here. The poem deals with time and space and the individual's fear when confronted with meaningful symbols of these two dimensions in which we live and move and have our being. Since ancient times, "since man hath been," two columns supporting golden eagles looking eastward have stood upon Mt. Lykaion, placed so that "the sun goes up between." From this height the poet looks downward, seeing a precarious balance of order and chaos:

> Far down around the mountain's oval green
> An order keeps the falling stones abreast.
> Below within the chaos last and least
> A river like a curl of light is seen.
> Beyond the river lies the even sea,
> Beyond the sea another ghost of sky,—

Confronted by all this, the soul feels a kind of terror, feels itself dwarfed and threatened, unable to maintain itself in the face of such immensities:

> O God, support the sickness of my eye
> Lest the far space and long antiquity
> Suck out my heart, and on this awful ground
> The great wind kill my little shell with sound.

Perhaps there was no direct influence, but one is reminded of a sentence from Pascal's *Pensées:* "The eternal silence of these infinite spaces terrifies me."[4] Insofar as "Mt. Lykaion" renders vividly a single conception, with no diverting subordinate themes, it is one of Stickney's finest achievements in the sonnet form.

"Lakeward" (1900), like "At Sainte-Marguerite" and the two "In Ampezzo" poems, concerns the change of season at autumn and two contrasting scenes. It is shortly before sunrise in an Italian mountain region. The poet feels tempted to lose his identity in this place, "Into your crystal winter/ To linger on unworlded and alone," but he has "the soul of a wayfarer!" As he begins to wander down the mountain, like the streams beginning their descent "lakeward," in search of "a sun-sweetened home," he wonders, "How long shall

---

4. *Pensées,* trans. Martin Turnell (New York: Harper, 1962), p. 221.

mountain iron and ice together/ Hold against summer-time."
As the journey southward continues, plant and vegetable life
slowly change, as do the streams themselves, until

> The outlines have a gentle meaning.
> Willows and clematis, foliage and grain!
> And the last mountain falls in terraces to the greening
> Infinite autumn plains.

The journey continues still, until "Sodden with sunlight,
green and gold, the country/ Suspends her fruit and stretches
ripe and still," while the river falls ever downward:

> The vale, the river and hills, that take
> The perfect south and here at last for ever
> Merge into thee, O Lake!—
>
> Sunset-enamored in the autumnal hours!

The poem concludes with a baroque-like personification of
sun and lake, while "a boat-load of labourers homeward
plashes,/ Singing 'Amor, Amor.' "

Some of the same themes may be seen in the two "In
Ampezzo" poems of 1898, the first of which is one of Stickney's finest and best-executed poems.[5] This poem opens with
a scene on the plain between Tofana and Cristallo. To the
south lie "lilac promontories/ Under green skies to Italy,"
while beyond Lavinores to the north there lies the Tyrol.
It is September and the time of harvest

> When scythes are swishing and the mower's muscle
> Spans a repeated crescent to and fro,
> Or in dry stalks of corn the sickles rustle,
> Tangle, detach and go,

---

5. The poem is "first" in that it appears earlier in the *Poems* of 1905 than
does the other with the same title.

although in the distance, "their heads of iron/ Sunken in sky whose azure overlights/ Ravine and edges," can be seen the "Desolate Dolomites." As "images of summer fade" the poet remembers past scenes of natural beauty: "A pine by sullen coasts, an oleander/ Reddening on the lake." (The reader should consult the chapter on the theme of time for a more detailed treatment of the functioning of memory in this poem.) The natural beauty will soon be ended, for "sheets of winter metal/ On this discoloured mountain-land will close." And, as "Summer and sunset-coloured autumn slowly/ Dissipate down the vale," the poet remembers that at sunrise, "A league above the moss and dying pines," he had picked a "parcel of columbines." Beauty has been found in a place of desolation. It will be recalled that this theme appears also in "At Sainte-Marguerite," and it is to be found in other poems as well, most explicitly in "The melancholy year is dead with rain."

The second poem with the title "In Ampezzo" is as a whole inferior to the first, though there are some fine things in it. The poet imagines himself on a summer day looking southward in the late afternoon. The poem contains a beautiful description of the scene as the poet looks in this direction:

> For evening there is lovelier
> Than vision or enchanted tale:
> When wefts of yellow vapour pale,
> And green goes down to lavender
> On rosy cliffs, shutting the vale
>
> Whose smoke of violet forest seeks
> The steep and rock, where crimson crawls,
> And drenched with carmine fire their walls
> Go thinly smouldering to the peaks,
> High, while the sun now somewhere falls;

> Except a cloud-caught ochre spark
> In one last summit . . .

The scene teems with life and color and sound throughout; and, with perhaps some echoes from Browning and Lanier, the poet wishes that he could capture, by means of a combination of the arts, this vision of beauty so that it might endure. Words alone are not sufficient, for "This world is better than an ode/ And evening more than elegy."

These, then, are the poems that are unified by means of landscape imagery. There are others which are in part so structured, but the focus ultimately turns to something else or shifts to landscape from another interest. Of more importance is the next kind of imagery to be considered.

ii. The Landscape of the Mind

Unlike the poems just discussed, which use landscape imagery throughout as a controlling metaphor or symbol, a great many of Trumbull Stickney's poems employ landscape imagery in a truly unique way. This imagery usually appears in a brief image within the compass of a line or two, occasionally more. The purpose of this imagery is to objectify emotions, attitudes, feelings—whatever one wishes to call it, it is in contrast to the rational, logical faculty of mind that analyzes along lines of dissection—and rarely it is also used to describe some aspect of the processes of thought itself. Although the phrase "the Landscape of the Mind" is applied here to this imagery, it must be understood that it is to include references not only to the mind but also to the brain, the soul, the heart, and so on, whichever is chosen as the seat of the emotions. One encounters this kind of imagery in a great number of Stickney's poems. It begins appearing about 1894, rather early in the writing career of a poet who did not live long anyway, and continues in some form or another until his death.

The imagery here called "the Landscape of the Mind" may be divided into four basic categories, although this procedure is obviously somewhat arbitrary. In the first category we find the focus upon imagery of land (and sometimes water as well). Most of this imagery in some way suggests either union or division.

First, examples of union: In "Kalypso" Ulysses is under the spell of the enchantress and addresses her at one point with these words:

> The life
> That spurred me thro' the waters of the world
> Was spent indeed,—and claimed again, O love,
> Upon thy soul's warm shore.

Kalypso's soul and the "warm shore" upon which Ulysses was cast have been fused into one image denoting safety and security. As befits the character of the Greek, however, despite his words he really longs for his home in faraway Ithaca. "In Summer" also contains imagery suggesting union, as well as other types to be examined later. In this poem the poet remembers an event from the past when he and his love made an excursion to "the donjon tower of old Gisors." At the beginning of this trip the mood is established:

> My heart's desolate meadow ways,
> All wet and green,
> Opened for her to wander in
> A little space.

The effect of this image should be obvious, and it is repeated in lines describing the two after their ascent to the tower,

where the view is of the "Sun-stricken prospect and the
dazzling air":

> And by her side
> Surely she saw my heart divide
> Like paradise
> For her to walk abroad in at noon-tide.

Such an experience in Stickney's poetry often "Reaches and
deepens and at last is wrought/ Into that life we are but do
not live"—that is, it becomes deeply imbedded in the mind
as a source of joy, sometimes of grief, depending on the nature of the experience. This beautiful octave from an untitled sonnet should serve to illustrate the idea:

> Your image walks not in my common way.
> Rarely I conjure up your face, recall
> Your language, think to hear your footstep fall
> In my lost home or see your eyes' sweet play.
> Rather you share the life that sees not day,
> Immured within the spirit's deep control,
> Where thro' the tideless quiets of the soul
> Your kingdom stretches far and far away.

One could scarcely find a better example of "the Landscape
of the Mind" than the last two lines.

Another example of land imagery suggesting union is a
rather unusual poem in which the poet imagines himself to
be a plant, and, by extension near the end of the poem, the
surrounding countryside. His love would seem to be the
entire environment upon which the plant is dependent: "I
also, where I stand within thy soul/ A plant of thine and
growing in thy year. . . ." If the season should cause the
plant's leaves to disappear so that nothing should prevent the
"Great darkness" from completely penetrating it, yet would
it maintain faith

> That at the end thou mightest repossess,
> Mightest possess again and further bless
> My sad and human acres, that are thine.

In this sonnet the plant is within the soul of the loved one, which by means of metaphor becomes everything necessary for its survival, but then the lover becomes not only a plant but "sad and human acres," sad, evidently, when not blessed.

"In a City Garden" is a poem in which the persona recalls an experience from the past, an experience when he and his loved one were together at some kind of holiday carnival. He has returned to find her, knowing that she would not be physically present, but more vividly present to memory: "Not in the acres of the Soul/ Does Nature drive the plough-share of her change."

Land imagery may also be used to suggest division. Two examples are to be found in the long sequence of related poems called "Eride," the sequence as a whole dealing with the development of a love affair and its ultimate breakup. Once the persona has realized that separation is inevitable, which realization either has not come to the other person or which she has not been willing to accept, we get this perhaps not entirely satisfying image:

> They say that love's a mustard seed
> Upon the acres of the heart;
> It spreads from one part like a weed
> To another part.
> Yet Spring is single and the days depart.

Elsewhere in "Eride" the speaker addresses his lover, explaining how, if they were together, there would be continual restlessness and in the end "solitude." These beautiful lines are used to describe the situation by analogy:

You know how, born by a small hearth,
While out in the sad dark it snows
And 't is for months an unseen earth,
The soul as by remembrance goes
After the warm vineyard and burning rose,

To live long years by stream and hill
Within the southern light, with men
Who speak delicious language:—till
The pain of being alien
Urges one elsewhere yet not home again.

A sonnet that deals with the desire for reconciliation begins "When I hereafter shall recover thee. . . ." Perhaps this reconciliation is to occur in the afterlife, since "eternity" is mentioned in the poem; such an interpretation is also suggested by the sea imagery, the journey to effect the reconciliation beginning from some "further margin." The possibility of such a future occurrence would seem to be questioned, however, by the phrase "if aught survive/ The raging wind and old disastrous sea." There is much in Stickney's poetry to suggest that he did not believe in the conventional notion of an afterlife, which is probably reflected in the despair that dominates the rest of the poem: "Sometimes I ask me why the morning sun/ Returns, or later, when the day is done,/ I let the dreams about my pillow strain." This despair is further expressed in the last three lines of the poem in which the interior world of the speaker is rendered vivid by "the Landscape of the Mind":

But then it sounds across my dying brain
Like torrents in the moonlight foaming on
Between enormous mountains to the plain.

This poem first appeared in *Dramatic Verses* of 1902, two years before Stickney's death from tumor of the brain; we should, therefore, be rather hesitant about attributing some aspects of it to his illness. There are, in addition, other poems which suggest this illness, and it is almost impossible not to read the fragment written shortly before his death which begins "Sir, say no more" as reflecting on his part an awareness of approaching death, whether such a reading be correct or not.

Another sonnet dealing with division has the traditional *carpe diem* theme and begins "When bye and bye relenting you regret/ All of these possible and vanished hours. . . ." This poem illustrates the fact that "the Landscape of the Mind" does not always reflect the interior world of the speaker but may be applied to another person, for the poem continues "And, rolling up, the certain tempest scours/ Your sky where not another star will set," the lines indicating the disappearance of the possibility of love.

At least two poems have lines that describe some aspect of the process of thought itself. One of these is entitled "Fidelity," and its third stanza is as follows:

> And o'er the imagination's last horizon
> No brain has leaning described nothing more:
> Still there are stars and in the night before
> More have arisen.

The second "In Ampezzo" poem, which has already been discussed, also contains a stanza dealing with contemplation. It occurs in the poem after the poet has described the beautiful scenes of the region and immediately before he expresses a desire to combine the arts in order to more fully capture and objectify the loveliness of this vision. It is thus a transitional stanza:

> And thoughts delicious of the whole,
> Gathering over all degrees,

> Yet sad for something more than these,
> Across low meadow-lands of soul
> Grow large, like north-lights no one sees.

One of the "Sonnets from Greece," entitled "Near Helikon," expresses melancholy, a kind of despair frequent in Stickney's verse. In contrast to the surroundings, where "all things together take their way/ Harmonious to the harvest" from the mountains to the sea, the poet reveals his own mood in lines that illustrate how brilliantly Stickney's poems, especally his sonnets, often end:

> To me my troubled life doth now appear
> Like scarce distinguishable summits hung
> Around the blue horizon: places where
> Not even a traveller purposeth to steer,—
> Whereof a migrant bird in passing sung,
> And the girl closed her window not to hear.

A sense of estrangement from all that makes life worth living could scarcely be rendered more effectively.

The second category of imagery under consideration here is characterized by light and darkness. It reflects two distinct moods, happiness and despair, the two of them appearing with almost equal frequency, although to make a distinction one must sometimes consider the context in which the imagery occurs.

The lovely "In Summer" has as its opening stanza the following:

> It's growing evening in my soul,
> It darkens in.
> At the gray window now and then
> I hear them toll
> The hour-and-day-long chimes of St. Etienne.

One must not, however, mistake the mood of this poem from these lines. The persona goes on to say immediately that "Indeed I'd not have lived elsewhere/ Nor otherwise," and the experience related in the poem, already discussed above, is one of happiness. The "evening in my soul" follows the course of the outer day and also suggests to some extent the process of aging, because the poem deals with memory and the value of past experience (see the chapter on the theme of time), the speaker concluding that "That time I lived the life I have." A less obvious example of light imagery is to be found in "Eride," when the persona describes in some of the most lyrical lines from that sequence of poems the beginning of the love affair. These lines illustrate "the Landscape of the Mind" only insofar as the eyes may be considered to reflect either the inner world of the lover or of the beloved:

> Your eyes, like flowers from apart
> Their frail and shaded gates of dream,
> Looked all a meadow's light astart
>
> With sunrise, and your smile did seem
> As when below a letting rain
> The water-drops with sunset gleam.

An untitled sonnet which begins with the line "You are to me the full vermilion rose" continues several lines later as follows:

> And while the rings of petal still disclose,
> My spirit likewise tenderly unbound
> Falls out in webs of shadow, and around
> The mercy of your beauty finds repose.

The poem as a whole is not entirely satisfactory, but the lines quoted are the best ones, a fact that may suggest what the

reader perhaps has already surmised, that Stickney writes best
when he employs "the Landscape of the Mind." It will also
be noted that this imagery is often used in association with
the theme of time and especially the functioning of memory.
Such is the case in the poem entitled "Ode," which describes
an incident high in the valley of Engadine when the poet has
an insight into something more than earthly, a vision of the
eternal processes of nature. This vision is to be retained by
the memory, so that it becomes part of the interior life:

> Farewell! again farewell!
> From where ye dwell
> We shall descend within the gentle plain,—
> There life is speakable:
> The while your train,
> In light of days that set not but still fare
> Upon the spirit's skies,
> More sober, more serene
> Shall rise,
> From all the things that were
> Apart,
> To that high backward of the heart
> Whereto the thought that travels ne'er hath wholly been.

The light/darkness imagery that reflects despair is of such
intensity that it usually stands out with great vividness in the
context in which it appears. Consider, for example, these
striking lines from "Eride," which occur when the persona
realizes that the love affair is doomed: "Cry on cry/ My
autumn's gone. A horrid blast/ Blows out my sunset from the
sky." Equally arresting is the first stanza from one of the
later undated lyrics, which again must make us think of
Stickney's approaching death. Although the season is spring
and the poet responds to the life of nature about him, ob-
serving "The eternal year disclose its heart of gold," there is

a sense of impending doom and a need for the reassurance
of love:

> With thy two eyes look on me once again.
> Since certain days, I know not how it is,
> I feel the swell of tidal darknesses
> Climb in my soul and overwhelm my brain.

One of the fragments published in the *Poems* of 1905 ends
with the ominous line " 'T is in my soul like midnight and
high tide." Another fragment, dated 1904, the year of Stickney's death, is as follows:

> Be patient, very patient; for the skies
> Within my human soul now sunset-flushed
> Break desperate magic on the world I knew,
> And in the crimson evening flying down
> Bell-sounds and birds of ancient ecstasy
> Most wonderfully carol one time more.

Considering the circumstances, R. P. Blackmur's singling
out of the last three lines of this fragment as what "might
have been written by almost any competent versifier in the
American nineties" seems extremely harsh criticism.[6] His
reasoning is that "the emotion is loose and drifting, the language vague, and the verse commonplace."[7] In reality, however, there is considerable pathos in the lines, since it is the
interior world Stickney is describing, "the skies/ Within my
human soul now sunset-flushed"; and the "crimson evening"
with its sounds are of the same world: they are the sounds
of poetry, a lovingly felt sense of inspiration in a man conscious of approaching death.

---

6. R. P. Blackmur, "Stickney's Poetry," *Poetry: A Magazine of Verse* 42
(June 1933) : 158.

7. *Ibid.*, pp. 158–59. For some reason, Blackmur focused upon the weaknesses of Stickney's poetry, almost entirely ignoring its merits.

In the dramatic poem entitled *Prometheus Pyrphoros* (1900), Pandora, pregnant by Zeus and possessed of more than mortal knowledge, begins her last song, immediately after Prometheus has been led away to his punishment, with these two stanzas which suggest that, as far as the beneficial aspects are concerned, the outer world is a projection of her spirit and is sustained in some mystical way by it:

> My soul of sunset every human day
> In long sad colours on the evening dwells
> And gives her solemn violet away
> Over the quiet endlessness of hills.
>
> Mild and gold burns from cloud to cloud, above
> The obscurer fields, my pity for an hour;
> And then life goes to sleep within my love,
> The world is drawn together as a flower.

The third category of imagery to be found in "the Landscape of the Mind" is derived from architecture, and it appears somewhat less frequently than the first two kinds discussed. This imagery is used in a few instances to convey a sense of separation or isolation. A stanza late in "Eride," when the persona has fully accepted the break-up of the relationship, will serve to illustrate this type:

> Sometimes I think we never met,
> Such immense walls of iron and ice
> Between us infinitely set
> Spring blind into the spirit's skies.

And one should not forget the closing lines of "Near Helikon," quoted above, in which a bird sings of a desolate, mountainous area (in actuality the poet's "troubled life"), "And the girl closed her window not to hear." The same kind of imagery may, however, be used to suggest a union of

spirits, as it does in the poem beginning "My friend, who
in this March unkind, uncouth. . . ." Here a youthful, idealistic friendship results in "building us archways unto Para-
dise/ Of all that greets the soul's all-flowering youth." Although this is a fairly early poem, it expresses a recurrent
theme: out of such experiences, even though they are forgotten by the mind, "from year to year and clime to clime/
Stretches the love that makes of all but one."

Architectural imagery may also be used to obtain a "spotlighted" effect. "Once" relates a moment of love now past
but remembered, as in so many other poems by this poet.
After an opening stanza in praise of the gracefulness of the
loved one ("She had the motion of the rose . . . She seemed
a wind of music passing on."), this "spotlighted" effect becomes evident: "Alone I saw her that one day/ Stand in the
window of my life." A less obvious example appears early
in "Eride" when the relationship between the two lovers
is still new. The persona brings a gift of tulips:

> I passed the love I bear you o'er
> Flower and stem.
> And I would leave them at your door,—
>
> If at your heart's door they might stand!
> Keeping awhile
> The world behind their petals and
> Crimson smile,—
> Like seas hid by a meadow-land.

The impressive sonnet "The melancholy year is dead with
rain" contains in its octave the best instance of this effect:

> The melancholy year is dead with rain.
> Drop after drop on every branch pursues.
> From far away beyond the drizzled flues
> A twilight saddens to the window pane.

> And dimly thro' the chambers of the brain,
> From place to place and gently touching, moves
> My one and irrecoverable love's
> Dear and lost shape one other time again.

One wonders how poetry as good as this could be so little known, even among historians of literature. It is surely an indication of our constant need to reclaim the past.

The fourth category of "the Landscape of the Mind" is more difficult to describe and, except in a few cases, is in some ways not so satisfying in the poetic image it produces as the other varieties. It does, however, appear with enough frequency in Stickney's poetry to warrant consideration. In addition, it illustrates Stickney's willingness to engage in some rather daring poetic strategy and is another indication of this poet's originality. There are two basic, contrasting types within this category. In the first, some inner emotion, usually love, is objectified—for example, as a flower springing from the soul. In the second, some object in the outer world or emotion in another person is absorbed by the poet's spirit; the face of a loved one or a token of her love would be examples.

In the first type, since the desire is for the soul to express itself, the result may be equal to poetry itself. This would seem to be the case in "Eride" in a passage in which the persona, while noticing an expression on the face of one person, is reminded of someone from the past. This linking of the present with the past is possible by "A colour, gesture, sound—a turn/ That makes the heart grow dull with rhymes/ And the soul's lips burn." The danger involved with the use of such a figure of speech is the resulting awkward personification. A more pleasing image with Biblical overtones appears in "Dear and rich as a dawn of summer":

> I've pressed thee a perfume of all my spirit
> And jewelled the twilight of my soul:
> O my darling, anoint thee! wear it!
> The days blow by and the seasons roll.

"Dedication" reveals quite clearly what happens with this type of imagery, the process of objectifying the inward: "Within my bosom blew this rose/ That on the moonlit autumn wind/ I toss to you. . . ." "A Stone" combines the sentimentality toward which Stickney tended with beautiful lines that express emotion concretely. The first stanza is an example of this combination and is also worthy of quoting because of its beautiful image:

> With burning hands and eyes all dull
> I bring to you this drop of fire,
> This topaz where the summerful
> Of August afternoons expire.

The stone was a gift from a loved one and has been worn around the neck:

> From thence I took it pure and whole
> To comfort me to-day, and found
> That from the waters of my soul
> These bands of gold have drawn around,
>
> This little setting's nervous art,

an image akin to "The frayed and dusty flowers of my soul" presented with "such belated show of sacrifice" in another poem, which is as unpleasing as "These daisies of my trembling spirit bred" (to be worn in the hair in place of a "crown of thorn") from another. In the youthful and imitative "Now with Return of Spring" (1894), "The rich fruit gathered

from the living years/ Of mind or soul" is to be dedicated
to the worship of Nature.

Better than this orchard imagery is the contrasting type,
that by which something from the outer world is absorbed
by the spirit of the speaker of the poem. An example comes
from one of the best poems in the sequence called "Eride,"
which begins as follows:

> Like a pearl dropped in red dark wine,
> Your pale face sank within my heart,
> Not to be mine, yet always mine.

The poem expresses the sense of miracle in youthful romantic
love: "I sang, and opened in your name/ Crocuses yellow
with moonrise." It continues to the realization that the love
affair is over, when "Nothing is left and all is past" and concludes by returning to the opening image:

> And as a pearl in red wine cast
> Glows like a drop of moonlight there,
> Your face possesses my despair.

A similar psychological effect is evident in "A Flower" and is
based upon the Narcissus myth:

> As kneeling at a water's edge
> Into my heart when I look down,
> Thy face uprising from the sedge
> Lies on the surface water-blown.

An anti-romantic might be tempted to say that it is just this
element of Narcissism that is the weakness of Romantic love
and poetry expressing it: the Romantic poet is seemingly
more interested in *his* reactions and emotions than in the
loved one, which perhaps accounts for much that is theatrical
in Romantic love poetry.

Related to this category of "the Landscape of the Mind" is the phenomenon by which the soul desires to free itself, to be caught up in some vision or ideal. In the Emperor Julian fragment, the Queen discusses the predicament of geniuses who, "their souls/ Strung for a brighter flight among the stars," have to live in a world of reality. Finally, the desire of the spirit to objectify itself is seen in the second of two poems entitled "Philosophies" that accompanied Stickney's undergraduate essay on Herakleitos, published in *The Harvard Monthly* in February of 1895. In this poem the persona is that of the life force, which seeks to express itself in ever-higher forms, culminating in intelligence:

> I chase one thought thro' many forms
> With more of heart than men suppose;
> My life is cast with kings and worms,
> Alike with thistle and with rose.
>
> The worn-out form is laid aside;
> Not having still I hope, I strain.
> . . . .
> For still mine early thought has grown
> Richer and fairer, and the day
> Glows brighter when, doubt overthrown,
> My thought shall glisten into clay.

Such then is "the Landscape of the Mind." Like the theme of time in Trumbull Stickney's poetry, it has been completely ignored, another indication of how poorly critics have read his verse, when they have taken the trouble to examine it at all. "The Landscape of the Mind" contains great potential as a poetic device, especially in the form of land, light/darkness, and architectural imagery, for it represents a new way of broadening the possibilities of the poet's expressing the relationship between his inner world and the outer world of experience. It is worthy of note that in the past few years a number of popular songs have employed a kind of imagery very similar to "the Landscape of the Mind." As poetic formulas and genres become worn with time, such new means of expression are of extreme importance, especially in a period, like our own, when the complexities of life have turned many a would-be poet to the more versatile and flexible medium of prose.

Trumbull Stickney's knowledge of ancient and of the modern literature of his own day was extensive. His father was a professor of Greek and Latin, and he himself studied the classics at Harvard. He also knew Sanskrit, but landscape has been used in other ways in the literature of that language,[8] the study of which he continued in Paris. Despite his intimacy with these languages, "the Landscape of the Mind" is not derived from their literature. It is also difficult to make a good case for its having come from one of the modern languages Stickney knew so well. The most logical choice among these would be French, but if it provided any influence it would apparently be the result of the poet's developing a new technique from something as rare as Verlaine's *Clair de lune*, which has the following as its opening stanza:

> *Votre âme est un paysage choisi*
> *Que vont charmant masques et bergamasques,*
> *Jouant du luth, et dansant, et quasi*
> *Tristes sous leurs déguisements fantasques.*

This kind of imagery is really unusual in Verlaine's poetry and in that of the period, and at best it could have provided only a germinal idea. It would seem more reasonable to assume, in the absence of evidence to the contrary, that "the Landscape of the Mind" is Trumbull Stickney's own original

8. See O. C. Gangoly, *Landscape in Indian Literature and Art* (University of Lucknow, 1963) , pp. 15–49.

creation. His frequent use of it and the often striking effect produced by it is surely evidence of poetic genius of an unusual nature, one that, had he lived beyond his short span of years, might have produced work of undisputed greatness. As it is, his poetry contains enough of the unusual blended in with Romantic poetic practices of a recognizable kind that it is the latter that has received attention. Such a state of affairs is, of course, not so much Stickney's fault as the fault of his critics. It is the result of a blending of the old with the new, the new passing unnoticed by eyes expecting to see something else. The following fragment written shortly before Stickney's death in 1904 has impressed several critics, perhaps for morbid reasons; and yet, as this chapter has attempted to make abundantly clear, it is not really such an unusual product of Stickney's pen:

> Sir, say no more.
> Within me 't is as if
> The green and climbing eyesight of a cat
> Crawled near my mind's poor birds.

7

The Theme of Time

Trumbull Stickney had a pronounced interest—perhaps it amounted to an obsession—in time; there are only a few of his poems in which this interest is not found.[1] It is somewhat surprising that the importance of this recurrent theme has escaped critical attention. This concern with time expresses itself in many ways and is quite evident in poems written during the Harvard undergraduate years before the long stay in Paris, where such ideas would have been encountered more frequently. The most conspicuous time-theme has to do with the effect of the past upon the present—its ability to provide consolation in the midst of a troubled present through recall of experiences and images; this theme develops into a romantic aestheticism and is found in some of Stickney's best poems. But the poet was too much of a realist to ignore that other side of the coin: memories of past experiences can sometimes cause us sorrow in the present,

1. This chapter is based upon my article "The Dust of Seasons: Time in the Poetry of Trumbull Stickney," *The Sewanee Review* 74 (Autumn 1966) : 899–914.

because either a state of achieved happiness has been lost forever, or an opportunity for happiness has been lost. Through the uses of memory, then, the past constantly modifies the present.

There are a number of poems dealing with man's awareness, within the limitations of time, of the eternal, his difficulty in perceiving it, and the necessity for him to attempt to transcend his finite vision of reality. In contrast to these are a few poems which urge acceptance of the present in a traditional *carpe diem* manner. In general, however, only the past and the eternal seem real in Stickney's poetry. The present seems chaotic and troubled; if there is any joy in the present it is derived from either the past or the eternal. The future is for the most part ignored, as though the poet were incapable of comprehending it. Probably because of his background in the classics, his familiarity with many lands, and his knowledge of the literature of the East, Stickney contrasts the manner in which time may be viewed within various cultures in a small but important group of poems. Finally, there are a number of poems dealing with many facets of time that fail to fall into convenient categories. The rest of this chapter will concern itself with a detailed exploration of the many aspects of time in the poetry of Trumbull Stickney.

i. The Uses of Memory and the Eternal Moment

Stickney's poems dealing with the effect of the past upon the present fall into three major categories—poems of grief, of consolation, and of "simultaneity." These three groups include several of the poet's finest lyrics. The poems of grief will be discussed first, because the poems of consolation represent, in a sense, a further thematic development and the growth of Stickney's aestheticism, while the poems of simultaneity illustrate a concern with the metaphysics of time.

In the poems of grief, memories of past sorrow or the loss of happiness prey upon the mind of the speaker of the poem. In "Once" we are presented with the climactic meeting of two lovers, which has been followed by an unexplained separation, the cause of present sorrow. The title is indicative of the ephemeral nature of the relationship, which is also subtly suggested in the first stanza:

> That day her eyes were deep as night.
> She had the motion of the rose,
> The bird that veers across the light,
> The waterfall that leaps and throws
> Its irised spindrift to the sun.
> She seemed a wind of music passing on.

The imagery of the poem is so arranged that the first two stanzas contrast with the third and fourth. The first two stanzas are characterized by imagery of light and the window and recall the past; the second two, by darkness and the shut doors of fate and represent the present. The poem concludes:

> If once again before I die
> I drank the laughter of her mouth
> And quenched my fever utterly,
> I say, and should it cost my youth,
> 'T were well! for I no more should wait
> Hammering midnight on the doors of fate.

The uneven quality of this poem, especially the worn out Petrarchanisms, probably illustrates what R. P. Blackmur had in mind when he condemned the "adolescent stultification" of Stickney's verse.[2] It is significant, however, that the

---

2. "Stickney's Poetry," *Poetry: A Magazine of Verse* 42 (June 1933) : 161.

past is captured quite successfully in the poem; the poet seems unable to express the emotions of the present, even resorting to wrenching the syntax by using "glitters" as subject and "midnight" as what is first felt to be an object. In the poems in which Stickney uses the persona of the bereaved lover, he tends to revert to sentimentality; this is especially true of much of "Eride."

"Pity" is a far better poem than "Once" because the speaker of the poem becomes an observer and is able to avoid sentimentality:

> An old light smoulders in her eye.
> There! she looks up. They grow and glow
> Like mad laughs of a rhapsody
> That flickers out in woe.
>
> An old charm slips into her sighs,
> An old grace sings about her hand.
> She bends: it's musically wise.
> I cannot understand.
>
> Her voice is strident; but a spell
> Of fluted whisper silkens in—
> The lost heart in a moss-grown bell,
> Faded—but sweet—but thin.
>
> She bows like waves—waves near the shore.
> Her hair is in a vulgar knot—
> Lovely, dark hair, whose curves deplore
> Something she's well forgot.
>
> She must have known the sun, the moon,
> On heaven's warm throat star-jewels strung—
> It's late. The gas-lights flicker on.
> Young, only in years, but young!
>
> One might remind her, say the street

> Is dark and vile now day is done.
> But would she care, she fear to meet—
> But there she goes—is gone.

The person observed, "the lost heart in a moss-grown bell," has been strangely aged by some unfortunate experience, "Something she's well forgot." Though young in years she now meets life as it comes, having been hardened by her experience. The poem strongly suggests that she is a prostitute. She has lost the spontaneity proper to youth, and for this reason the narrator pities her.

The sonnet "On Some Shells Found Inland" is similar to "Pity" in that the poet attempts to maintain objectivity, in this case by endowing the shells with memories of happier times:

>   Shall they forever feel
> Glories undone and worlds that cannot be?—
> 'T were mercy to stamp out this agèd wrong,
> Dash them to earth and crunch them with the heel
> And make a dust of their seraphic song.

The past tortures us by making us feel "Glories undone and worlds that cannot be."

"Eride" is a loosely knit series of lyrics of varying quality dealing with the course of an unsuccessful love from its beginning in the spring to its breakup in the late fall. The object of this love seems to be a passionate bluestocking incapable of a permanent, satisfactory relationship. The speaker realizes that his love has been illusory:

> It comes to only a memory.
> We have too many memories,
> And somehow I believe we die
> Of things like these,
> Loving what was not, might not be, nor is.

The speaker continues by describing the effect of this realization upon him through a striking image:

> Cry on cry
> My autumn's gone. A horrid blast
> Blows out my sunset from the sky.
>
> Nothing is left and all is past;

even though in the winter of this love "The soul as by remembrance goes/ After the warm vineyard and burning rose," too much has happened in the "unalterably separate past" for the relationship to be continued. The poem concludes with the speaker desiring to become part of nature.

Often the ability of memory to re-create the past is not satisfactory in itself; instead it increases desire for that which can no longer be. As a sad violinist attempts to comfort himself with "some persuasion born of long ago,"

> So with thy picture I alone devise,
> Passing on thy uncoloured face the tone
> Of memory's autumnal paradise . . .

In the poems dealing with grief caused by memories of unfortunate experiences, Stickney found it difficult to avoid sentimentality, as we have noted. The more successful of these poems transfer the emotion felt to another person or object. In general, the poems centering on memory that end with a sense of consolation are superior to this group.

The poems of consolation are usually marked by a serenity the result of which was to enable Stickney to maintain better control of his materials. Some aspects of the poet's use of the past seem akin to that of the "Condillacian being" of the eighteenth century, as described by Georges Poulet:

it is a consciousness whose interior progress constitutes a life and a history. Each new moment of awareness reveals two distinct features: not only the new sensation which is the kernel of the moment, but also the ensemble of sensations already lived, whose resonances prolong themselves within it and surround it with their nebula. . . . By remembering, man escapes the purely momentary; by remembering, he escapes the nothingness that lies in wait for him between moments of existence.[3]

"In a City Garden" illustrates this idea. The speaker has returned to the scene of a meeting with a lover, which presumably took place some time ago in a city garden then decorated for a festival (the exact location of the scene is not specified, but details referring to the Orient suggest the East). The garden seems to have changed during the years, for "here the Past has left no residue." It occurs to the speaker that

> Many like me
> Loiter perhaps as I in after years,
> As looking here to see
> Some vestige of the living that was theirs,
> Some trace of yesterday,
> Some hint or remnant, echo, clue . . .

Yet "Love that disbelieves the real years" that have passed is capable of reliving the past in its original intensity. The moment of the meeting of the lovers amid the "gold bazars" [*sic*] is recalled, and we are told how "love across our eyes/ Broke with the sun." The wares of the bazaar and the bright colors of the natives are presented in considerable detail, because, it would seem, they provide the necessary background for the support of memory. The narrator has returned to find his lover, knowing she would not be there, but he has nevertheless been consoled by recalling the original experience:

3. *Studies in Human Time*, trans. Elliott Coleman (Baltimore: The Johns Hopkins Press, 1956), pp. 23–24.

Not in the acres of the Soul
Does Nature drive the ploughshare of her change.
It is not strange
That here in part and whole
The faithful eye sees all things as before.
For past the newer flowers,
Above the recent trees and clouds come o'er,
Love finds the other hours
Once more.

The first piece called "In Ampezzo" in the *Poems* is rightly
considered one of Stickney's finest poetic achievements. It
belongs to a whole series of landscape poems in which the
scenes described represent complex states of mind. In this
one, the speaker describes the plain between Tofana and
Cristallo and the surrounding area during the autumn:

Only once more and not again—the larches
Shake to the wind their echo, "Not again,"—
We see, below the sky that over-arches
Heavy and blue, the plain

Between Tofana lying and Cristallo
In meadowy earths above the ringing stream:
Whence interchangeably desire may follow,
Hesitant as in dream,

At sunset, south, by lilac promontories
Under green skies to Italy, or forth
By calms of morning beyond Lavinores
Tyrolward and to north:

As now, this last of latter days, when over
The brownish field by peasants are undone
Some widths of grass, some plots of mountain clover
Under the autumn sun . . .

From the scenes of harvest may be seen the surrounding
mountains:

Whilst high around and near, their heads of iron
Sunken in sky whose azure overlights
Ravine and edges, stand the gray and maron [*sic*]
Desolate Dolomites,—

And older than decay from the small summit
Unfolds a stream of pebbly wreckage down
Under the suns of midday, like some comet
Struck into gravel stone.

Here in September "images of summer fade," but the "pris-
tine/ Viols" of memory evoke other images

Of many a place where lovingly we wander,
More dearly held that quickly we forsake,—
A pine by sullen coasts, an oleander
Reddening on the lake.

This action of the memory is somewhat similar to that of
Rousseau and other Romantics in that

a present object, by the association of resemblance, recalls the
image of an object of the past, which, in its turn, by the association of contiguity, causes the awakening of feelings. Whatever the worth of this associationist psychology, in any case
there is no doubt that the affective memory needs the assistance
of the ordinary memory, or at least, the help of a recollecting
sign, and that the two memories are always inextricably mixed.[4]

Thus the storehouse of memory brings the past to bear upon
present perception:

From many easts the morning gives her splendour;
The shadows fill with colours we forget;
Remembered tints at evening grow tender,
Tarnished with violet.

But the speaker wishes to flee the scene because

---

4. *Ibid.,* p. 179.

soon sheets of winter metal
On this discoloured mountain-land will close,
While elsewhere Spring-time weaves a crimson petal,
Builds and perfumes a rose.

There are two alternatives, either to leave the scene or

To follow some diviner monotone,
And in all beauties, where ourselves commingle,
Love but a love, but one,

that is, to accept beauty wherever it might be found.
Here, at the change of seasons, the mountains stand in contrast to the plains:

past yon dumb and melancholy
Sameness of ruin, while the mountains ail,
Summer and sunset-coloured autumn slowly
Dissipate down the vale;

And all these lines along the sky that measure
Sorapis and the rocks of Mezzodì
Crumble by foamy miles into the azure
Mediterranean sea:

Whereas to-day at sunrise, under brambles,
A league above the moss and dying pines
I picked this little—in my hand that trembles—
Parcel of columbines.

Like the "oleander/ Reddening on the lake," the columbines found high in the mountains will be retained by the memory as an image capable of furnishing delight.[5] This interpretation of "In Ampezzo" may be supported by a comparison with "The melancholy year is dead with rain," the sestet of

---

5. For a quite different interpretation, see Thomas Riggs, Jr., *Trumbull Stickney (1874–1904)* (Princeton dissertation, 1949), pp. 127–31. Far from being a failure of nerve and "a sign pointing to an unspecified emotion," the next to the last line is the key to the poem.

which seems to echo the experience of the former poem with its "parcel of columbines":

> So in the last of autumn for a day
> Summer or summer's memory returns.
> So in a mountain desolation burns
> Some rich belated flower, and with the gray
> Sick weather, in the world of rotting ferns
> From out the dreadful stones it dies away.

This same motif appears in the companion sonnets entitled "Chestnuts in November."

The other "In Ampezzo" poem describes the same autumn scene as its companion piece but focuses upon the inadequacy of any one art to capture the experience. The solution is to

>   musically bear
> The burden of the gathered arts
> Together which divided were,
>
> And, passing Knowledge, highly rear
> Upon her iron architrave
> These airy images we rave,—
> Lest wholly vain and fallen sheer
> Our vision dress us for the grave.

Thus, to fail to capture the vision of beauty is to suffer a kind of death. One feels that Stickney's need to retain memories of beauty was urgent, since scarcely any other consolation is offered in his poetry. The early "Verses" (published in January of 1893) explains that "summer dies,/ Yet, dying, sends the memory of her sway/ Into the later skies" and takes solace in the knowledge that "Not fully yet is dead beyond reclaim/ The past. . . ." These poems are similar in some ways to Wordsworth's "I Wandered Lonely as a Cloud" and "Tintern Abbey."

Memory and the imagination sometimes free the roaming
spirit that characterizes so much of Stickney's poetry:

> Tho' inland far with mountains prisoned round,
> Oppressed beneath a space of heavy skies,
> Yet hear I oft the far-off water-cries
> And vague vast voices which the winds confound.
> . . . .
> Alone upon the shore in the wet light
> I stand, and hear the infinite sea that calls.

Another group of poems takes as its theme the tendency
of the imagination to obliterate the distinctions of time in
order to make a kind of eternity within duration. William F.
Lynch, S.J., writes of this phenomenon as follows:

> A principal mode of attack on the movement of time and the
> finiteness of human reality can be described under the heading
> of "simultaneity." The term covers the impulse to pack the
> past and the future, indeed the whole of scattered being, into
> the present moment—thus to possess all things in a single in-
> stant and to demolish the narrow gates of both space and time.[6]

Father Lynch cites Proust, Baudelaire, Poe, and Descartes
as examples of writers who employ simultaneity. This desire
to transcend time by enriching it takes two forms in Stickney's poetry: sometimes emphasis is upon the present moment and, as might be expected, at other times it is upon a
short period of time in the past, which is given its importance
through its influence upon the present. "In Summer" will
serve to illustrate the latter type. The poem opens at the
close of day:

> It's growing evening in my soul,
> It darkens in.

6. *Christ and Apollo, The Dimensions of the Literary Imagination* (New
York: Sheed and Ward, Inc., 1960), p. 34.

At the gray window now and then
I hear them toll
The hour-and-day-long chimes of St. Etienne.

Indeed I'd not have lived elsewhere
Nor otherwise, . . .

The reverie continues with "the fancy shaking out her sail":

My heart's desolate meadow ways,
All wet and green,
Opened for her to wander in
A little space.
I'd have it even so as it has been.

Finally, the event that forms the nucleus of the poem is given:

It seems to me I might stoop down to kneel

In memory of that day in June
When, all the land
Lying out in lazy summer fanned
Now and anon
By dying breezes from the Channel strand,

With nothing in our lives behind,
Nothing before,
In sunlight rich as melting ore
And wide as wind
We clomb the donjon tower of old Gisors

Thro' the portcullis botched in wood
And up, in fear,
A laddered darkness of a stair,
Up to the good
Sun-stricken prospect and the dazzling air.—

Even now I shade my breaking eyes.—
And by her side

> Surely she saw my heart divide
> Like paradise
> For her to walk abroad in at noon-tide.
>
> It swims about my memory.

The occasion has been reproduced as on a photograph, with its light/darkness and stairway imagery. That moment has transcended the limitations of ordinary time:

> That time I lived the life I have:
> A certain flower
> Blooms in a hundred years one hour,
> And what it gave
> Is richer, no, nor more, but all its power.
>
> The chimes are ended for to-day.
> After midnight
> Solitude blows her candle out;
> Dreams go away,
> And memory falls from the mast of thought.

Thus the chimes, which served to initiate the series of memories, also serve to end them.

"Fidelity" expresses the permanence of the relationship indicated by the title:

> Thy eyes it seems upon my eyes did shine
> Since forever.
> .   .   .   .
>
> Not won or lost is unto thee my being;
> Our eyes were always so together met.
> If mine should close, if ever thine forget,
> Time is dying.

In this group of poems it is not chronological time that is important, but rather existential time:

My life shall count by the smile and tear,
    By the flash of blue in an eye I know.
It's a world of time since June last year
    And a timeless world I am living now.

. . . .

Dear love, what a trick Time plays on us!—
    As tho' the hour and day could give
A rule for passage! or all this fuss
    Of the sun be measure how long we live!

Life is older than all the aeons;
    And younger than any moment, youth.
For aught that the earth go gathering seasons
    The fact o' the Spring is the world's best truth.

The turn in phrasing with "world" and "time" is character-istic of a number of passages in Stickney's poetry that remind one of a modern poet such as Dylan Thomas. The last line quoted could have been written by E. E. Cummings.

If love can conquer time, the lover can return to the scene of past unhappiness which,

Since first you, darling, called my spirit yours,
Seem happy, and the gladness pours
From day to day,
And yester-year across this year endures
Unto next year away.

. . . .

And all the movement of the natural hours
Turns into melody.
           ("Loneliness")

As we have seen thus far, the past weighed heavily upon Stickney's mind and furnished inspiration for a good many poems. Memories of unhappy experiences in general, or the use of a persona indicating such experiences, seem to have been felt too deeply for the poet to express them with proper control, the result being a tendency to lapse into sentimentality. Those poems in which the past is relived by the memory because of some happy occurrence, and those in which an image capable of evoking aesthetic satisfaction is added to the reservoir of memory, are marked by a serenity and control that allowed for greater artistic achievement. Finally, Stickney's concern with the felt quality of experiences, often occurring in the past, led him to an attempt to destroy the normal boundaries of time in order to make existence more meaningful.

ii. The Fright of Time and the Vision of Eternity

Stickney's concern with time was not limited to the ability of memory to re-create the past, or to simultaneity. It may be seen in a variety of poems that, taken together, reveal an imagination returning again and again to the same theme but approaching it from different points of view. Time is the most important theme in Stickney's poetry; there are only a few poems having no relation to this theme. The remainder of the poems to be discussed in this chapter tend to fall into one or another of the following groups: those which examine time from a cultural standpoint; those which show a fear of time; those which reveal a concern with the possibilities open to man within the course of time; and those in which time is transcended through a vision of the eternal.

In three poems Stickney dealt with time from the standpoint of culture and history. Two of these, "Oneiropolos" and the "Emperor Julian" fragment, focus upon periods of cultural transition that provide a contrast between the old and the new.

"Oneiropolos" is a dramatic monologue about the decay
of Athens. Oneiropolos is an Indian who has come to Athens
as a result of Alexander's conquest of the East. He is a "seller
of dreams"; that is, he tells fortunes, using cards and birds.
The Athenians, who think of their town as the whole civilized
world, are living in a kind of afterglow of their golden age.
Oneiropolos tells of his experiences in India under his guru,
Brihadashua,

> Who dwelt in Kashi by the holy stream.
> Happy indeed was I, happy to count
> A wizard in my kindred such as he,
> Whose lips were wholly dedicate to truth,
> Whose hand dispensed serene and wonderful
> Peace to the spirit as a tree his shade.

Brihadashua taught his disciples that conquest of self characteristic of Indian philosophy:

> Continually did fall
> The pleasant dew of patience from his eye,
> Which looking ever beyond world and star
> Was large as upper heaven. They were the days
> When I had laid the world to rest within me. . . .

Having been caught up in the movement of people that
was the result of Alexander's dominion of the East, Oneiropolos came to Athens,

> This Grecian race of laughter, pleasure, song.
> Pity, nor giving alms, nor anything
> That makes the spirit pure, is here. They live,
> And suffer the forgetfulness of life.

It is

> A dying town filled of a feeble race,

Small gossips of their all-expressing tongue,
Dancers and frolickers, philosophers
Drunken and sense-tied to the trembling world.

. . . .

For they count Time upon their nervous hand.

Men come from all over the world to see the monuments of former Athenian glory:

But all is gone.
'T is vision, tale of poets, memory, nothing;
Now there is void shadow, blown by wind,
And the unstoried year is rolled away.

Here in the dying town I sell them dreams . . .

The "rose and glory of their world" is Phryne, the famous prostitute, who "hovers mothlike round her destiny;/ For all her wings and beauty are for sale." The one person in Athens who has that sense of inner calm typical of Oriental thought is Epicurus, "for many hear/ The spoken solace of his quietude." Oneiropolos and Epicurus have both achieved mastery of self by transcending the temporal.

A parallel to "Oneiropolos" may be seen in the twenty-four page "Emperor Julian" fragment, in that two cultures are again contrasted. Julian, whose brother Gallus has just been put to death because of atrocities he committed while ruling the East, is suspected of being a heretic and perhaps plotting for the throne. He is brought before Constance, the Emperor, and questioned concerning his religious beliefs. In contrast to the concern with pomp in the Christian court, Julian's interest is in men who are ironically

Merely philosophers and pagan priests,
Who in the brain's high nonsense are embarked
On seas of error, wastes of speculation,
After the quest and mirage of the truth.

It will be Julian's mission as Emperor to attempt to reverse
the processes of time, to revive the "dull ideals of an extin-
guished world."

Prometheus Pyrphoros, Stickney's most extended piece of
poetic writing, is a dramatic scene of almost seven hundred
lines. As the story opens, darkness covers the earth because
Prometheus has tricked Zeus. The reactions of the characters to their situation represent the major views one might
take toward the plight of existence. As was remarked in an
earlier chapter, Prometheus, who represents heroic struggle,
steals fire from heaven but is punished for his act. Pandora's
part in this drama is rather strange. Being with child by Zeus,
she stands apart singing at intervals as though unaffected by
the course of events. She seems to have an understanding of
the wider scheme of things:

> Yet I look further over larger ways.
> For pity is not of that nor this,
> And kindness stretches out her arm
> On all that is,
> To keep the grass-blade and the star from harm.

As these poems illustrate, Stickney's study of Eastern philosophy had a strong bearing on his wider view of time. However, a far greater number of lyrics suggest that in his personal
life he too felt "time's wingèd chariot hurrying near."

One of Stickney's most powerful poems on time is the
following:

> Leave him now quiet by the way
> To rest apart.
> I know what draws him to the dust alway
> And churns him in the builder's lime:
> He has the fright of time.

I heard it knocking in his breast
A minute since;
His human eyes did wince,
He stubborned like the massive slaughter beast
And as a thing o'erwhelmed with sound
Stood bolted to the ground.

Leave him, for rest alone can cure—
If cure there be—
This waif upon the sea.
He is of those who slanted the great door
And listened—wretched little lad—
To what they said.

This poem, which relates a traumatic initiation into an awareness of the consequences of time, including death, perhaps explains the poet's intense preoccupation with this theme.

Not only is there fear of the future ever impinging upon the present; there is also an awareness of the past, to which we are bound as prisoners:

There lies a somnolent lake
Under a noiseless sky,
Where never the mornings break
Nor the evenings die.

. . . .

The rocks rise sheer and gray
From the sedgeless brink to the sky
Dull-lit with the light of pale half-day
Thro' a void space and dry.

And the hours lag dead in the air
With a sense of coming eternity
To the heart of the lonely boatman there:
That boatman am I . . .
("In the Past")

The boat is "Lapped in the sweep of a sluggish tide/ Crawled in from the living sea," the living sea being that portion of time which is not past. The rocks surrounding the lake

> lie like walls of a circling urn
> Wherein lie bound
>
> The waters that feel my powerless strength
> And meet my homeless oar
> Labouring over their ashen length
> Never to find a shore.

The poem, obviously in the Poe style of imagery, reveals how one lives on in the frozen permanence of the past. "The heart is alive" there because a vital part of one's being is determined by the past, which extends into the present and seems an eternity. In "Lodovico Martelli" the dying poet laments, "How large a burial is the Past!" And, in "Kalypso," Ulysses, prisoner of the enchantress, is "vexed by incessant memory and recall" of faraway Ithaca.

Faced with this dual dilemma of past and future, there are two alternatives: one can live for the moment or practice resignation, as suggested by two often-anthologized poems. The first choice is rendered as follows:

> Live blindly and upon the hour. The Lord,
> Who was the Future, died full long ago.
> . . . .
> Thou art divine, thou livest,—as of old
> Apollo springing naked to the light,
> And all his island shivered into flowers.

Or one can

> Be still. The Hanging Gardens were a dream
> That over Persian roses flew to kiss

The curlèd lashes of Semiramis.
Troy never was, nor green Skamander stream.
Provence and Troubadour are merest lies.
The glorious hair of Venice was a beam
Made within Titian's eye. The sunsets seem,
The world is very old and nothing is.
Be still. Thou foolish thing, thou canst not wake,
Nor thy tears wedge thy soldered lids apart,
But patter in the darkness of thy heart.
Thy brain is plagued. Thou art a frighted owl
Blind with the light of life thou'ldst not forsake,
And Error loves and nourishes thy soul.

Perhaps the youth who had "the fright of time" is the same
one who sees the aged as a contamination of nature in "Age in
Youth":

> From far she's come, and very old,
> And very soiled with wandering.
> The dust of seasons she has brought
> Unbidden to this field of Spring.

The old hag's journey through the fields toward the setting
sun is seen as a "scar upon the year."

At least one poem suggests that nature loses its vital essence
through the course of time. The persona of "The immortal
mixes with mortality" would appear to be a being whose
memory encompasses a history old as man:

> I do remember greater worlds than these,
> An earth less arrogant, and higher hills.
> .   .   .   .
> Now nature fills with waning. One by one
> Monster and centaur die, . . .
> Alas! and we! indeed we somehow pass
> Within a fatal evening of ourselves.
> I feel a time-like tremor in my limbs.

It is the fear of time and of death that sets man apart from all other creatures, which accept the limitations of life in sheer animal ignorance; but in the case of man we "read on polished graves the little cry/ Of this delirious immortality!" ("In a Churchyard"). Yet this is an illusion, for

> the last day being come, Man stood alone
> Ere sunrise on the world's dismantled verge,
> Awaiting how from everywhere should urge
> The Coming of the Lord. And, behold, none
> Did come,

and, as the last man dies,

> Low in the East now lighting gorgeously
> He saw the last sea-serpent iris-mailed
> Which, with a spear transfixèd, yet availed
> To pluck the sun down into the dead sea.

If the ultimate future holds no promise for man, as this apocalyptic vision suggests, it does not follow that there is nothing of value within its course. Man still has his dreams. He may, like Lodovico Martelli, the poet who died before he had a chance to write all the poems he *felt,* have

> thought
> To have plucked the yellow comets by their hair,
> To have braided meteors, and from 'hind the moon
> Robbed her society of chanting tides.

Dream and intention are all-important, for

> Completed earth's a leaf
> Turning in space along with the other dust
> That blinds the eye of God.

As the "Fragment of an Ode for Greek Liberty" states,

> It needs not to have won
> To be great.
> But the exulting soul
> Which strides alone against the sun,
> By his own passion hurled
> And slave to his desire's supreme control
> Is master of the world.

Man may be defeated, but there is still nobility in the heroic struggle, an idea that appears with some frequency in Stickney's verse. "Tho' lack of laurels and of wreaths not one" pits an unconquerable "fate" against the human lot but insists that "a purpose never is undone,"

> And here while all the lowering heaven is ringed
> With our loud death-shouts echoed, on the field
> Stands forth our Nikè, proud, tho' broken-winged.

If, then, there is still value in life besides the aesthetic delight in nature's images, which the memory retains, it is made possible through the processes of time, as the following sonnet suggests:

> These are the strings of the Aegean lyre
> Across the sky and sea in glory hung:
> Columns of white thro' which the wind has flung
> The clouds and stars, and drawn the rain and fire.
> Their flutings now to fill the note's desire
> Are strained and dubious, yet in music young
> They cast their full-blown answer far along
> To where in sea the island hills expire.
> How bravely from the quarry's earthen gloom
> In snow they rose amid the blue to stand
> Melodious and alone on Sunium!
> They shall not wither back into the land.
> The sun that harps them with his golden hand
> Doth slowly with his hand of gold consume.

The columns, which are all that remain of the Greek temple, still represent the glory of the past, even as they are being destroyed: beauty and destruction are integral aspects of the processes of time.

As "Song" tells us, with its alternative refrains between the linnet (the heart) and the cuckoo (the brain), time can be apprehended only by the heart, or intuition, not by the understanding.[7]

Stickney's concern with time led him, as we have seen, to reject the orthodox Christian view of the course of history, especially the concept of the Second Coming. However, he was not content with a mere denial of the traditional Western view of the course of time. There are other alternatives, one of them naturalistic, perhaps pantheistic:

> I love to see the rolling sod
> Mixing and changing ever grow
> To other forms,—and this is God
> And all of God and all we know.
> > ("Driftwood")

After death one can return to "the dark matter that is life."

Man, the temporary inhabitant of a planet in the vast universe, is awed by "far space" and "long antiquity," as "Mt. Lykaion" so dramatically illustrates; this sonnet shows the juxtaposition in nature of order and chaos, space and time. The inquiring mind is naturally brought to look for something of permanence from which it will derive psychological security; the "Mt. Ida" sequence of sonnets explores this theme. Mt. Ida, the place where the infant Zeus was hidden from his father Cronus, becomes a symbol of permanence, difficult to see because of the clouds that hide it.

---

7. Cf. Henri Bergson, *Introduction to Metaphysics,* trans. T. E. Hulme (New York: The Liberal Arts Press, 1955), pp. 46–49, *et passim.*

The mountains slumber seaward sanctified,
And cloudy shafts of bluish vapour hide
The places where a sky and world have been.
O Ida, snowy bride that God espoused
Unto that day that never wholly is,
Whiten thou the horizon of my eyes,
That when the momentary sea aroused
Flows up in earthquake, still thou mayest rise
Sacred above the quivering Cyclades.

Although it is difficult to attain the vision of the eternal, man
must nevertheless struggle for this vision:

Is it the rule of all things infinite
To trail across remoteness and in clouds
The glory of their sacerdotal shrouds,
And shade with evening their eternal light?
O travellers abroad the mortal plain
On weary beasts of burden overta'en
By the unspeakable hours, I say: Press on.
For tho' a little part be hardly seen,
Hope spangles out the rest, and while ye strain
Another cloud already, look, is gone.

"Ode," one of Stickney's finest poems, is a brilliant statement of the vision of eternity (the poem has been strangely
ignored). The scene is the valley of Engadine, high in the
Swiss mountains. The poem opens with the poet bidding
farewell to the scene, to which he had come "Enlaced about
with human thought." It was here that the vision came to
him; the awe expressed is somewhat similar to that of "Mt.
Lykaion":

A terror spelled us at the windy lights;
Our breath grew lame
And on this world our vision fell distraught.
Too stinging near the sun!

The space too utter large! the air
Acrid so fine it was!
Our beaten spirit, impotent to share,
Became as glass
Brittle and dead before the vision:
We could our face but hide,
Our arms about us for a pall;
"Heaven has shattered us," we cried and cried.
Our ear dissolved; our voice quavered; and we were small.

At this point the vision centers on the order of "the rich passage of the natural days" and of the earth's "serene adjustment" amid the seeming confusion of its surface features, an insight that brings with it "The healing knowledge of eternal things." Here, before the eternal, man loses his sense of time: "Ye enfolded us and we did lose/ The little habit of the hour and way." The vision is, of course, essentially religious in the Romantic tradition of nature worship:

So man may stand with open eye,
A dying acolyte
Amid your ceremonies that do not die;
And hear,
In sober and subduèd soul,
Without fear
The roll
And tidal motion of the sacramental air.

From the mountains the poet will descend into the plain, where "life is speakable." This poem is akin to the poems of consolation discussed above in that the experience will be retained by memory "In light of days that set not but still fare/ Upon the spirit's skies," and will rise "To that high backward of the heart/ Whereto the thought that travels ne'er hath wholly been."

Among the fragments Stickney left is one that is a philo-

sophic statement of the nature of time and probably represents the poet's final view. "The Soul of Time" tells us that

> Time's a circumference
> Whereof the segment of our station seems
> A long straight line from nothing into naught.

Thomas Riggs, Jr., has made the following observation:

> The linear concept of time—which had advised the dramatic
> structure of the Prometheus poem—. . . is resolved within the
> concept of the cycle, the Indic image of the wheel. The struc-
> ture of "progress" is not denied but reduced to its place within
> the cycle. It is a partial structure only, a segment, and not the
> whole.[8]

However, it is necessary to qualify this observation in several
respects. As pointed out elsewhere, *Prometheus Pyrphoros*
is not concerned fundamentally with progress or its denial.
"The Soul of Time" also insists that "the victories of faith/
Are soldiered none the less with certainties" and that those
who struggle toward a goal find themselves

> in the track of some discovery,
> The grip and cognizance of something true,
> Which won resolves a better distribution
> Between the dreaming mind and real truth.

Man, though he strives under the illusion of the straight line
of time, in achieving his goals comes nearer to the truth.

Time was of major concern to Stickney and provided a
unique point of focus for his poetic imagination. His intense
preoccupation with the theme of time makes his poetry highly
relevant to the modern sensibility.

Concentrating on the inner life of the spirit, the poet's

---

8. P. 265.

exploration of the effect of the past upon the present resulted in an aestheticism, such as is found in the first "In Ampezzo" poem, in which images of nature's beauties are retained by the memory and furnish consolation in the midst of the troubled present. Not content with this aestheticism, however, Stickney attempted to make time more meaningful by relating it, not to objective systems of measurement, but to its significance for the spirit of man. The result of this attempt was a fusion of the past, the present, and the future into a period of time marked by its emotional intensity; this simultaneity is found in "In Summer" and in other poems.

Stickney's general concern with time and his knowledge of classical and Eastern cultures led him to compare one culture with another in terms of its concepts of time. The poems of this kind, such as "Oneiropolos," indicate that his sympathies lay with those who can escape the turmoil of the present by realizing its relative insignificance in the full course of time or infinity. Regardless of this conclusion, however, poems such as "Leave him now quiet by the way" and "In the Past" show time to be a menace that the individual faces; this is true of the past, the present, and the future, about which Stickney is rather pessimistic. Nevertheless, a man is judged by the nobility he displays as he "strides alone against the sun."

If the temporal is seen against the background of the eternal, man has a truer view of the significance of his struggle, whether his ultimate end be to face annihilation or to become part of "the dark matter that is life." As the Mt. Ida sonnets and the brilliant "Ode" suggest, the eternal processes of nature are worthy of man's admiration and reverence. Thus, with full awareness of his place in the universe, man can maintain his dignity by striving for ideals and receiving comfort from the glories and permanence of nature.

Selected Bibliography

Adams, Henry. *The Education of Henry Adams, An Autobiog-raphy*. Boston and New York: Houghton Mifflin Company, 1927.

———. *Henry Adams and His Friends*. Edited by Harold Dean Cater. Boston: Houghton Mifflin Company, 1947.

———. *Letters of Henry Adams* (1892–1918). Edited by Worth-ington Chauncey Ford. Boston and New York: Houghton Mifflin Company, 1938.

———. *The Life of George Cabot Lodge*. Boston and New York: Houghton Mifflin Company, 1911.

Aiken, Conrad, ed. *American Poetry 1671–1928*. New York: The Modern Library, 1929.

———, ed. *Twentieth-Century American Poetry*. New York: Random House, Inc., 1944.

Baym, Max I. *The French Education of Henry Adams*. New York: Columbia University Press, 1951.

Bergson, Henri. *Introduction to Metaphysics*. Translated by T. E. Hulme. New York: The Liberal Arts Press, 1955.

Berthoff, Warner. *The Ferment of Realism, American Literature, 1884–1919*. New York and London: The Free Press, 1965.

Blackmur, R. P. "The American Literary Expatriate." In *Foreign Influences in American Life*. Edited by David F. Bowers. Princeton: Princeton University Press, 1944, pp. 126–45.

———. "Stickney's Poetry." *Poetry: A Magazine of Verse* 42 (June 1933) : 158–63.

Bogan, Louise. *Achievement in American Poetry 1900–1950.* Chicago: Henry Regnery Company, 1951.

Brooks, Van Wyck. *The Confident Years: 1885–1915.* New York: E. P. Dutton & Co., Inc., 1952.

————. *New England: Indian Summer, 1865–1915.* New York: E. P. Dutton & Co., Inc., 1940.

Brown, Maurice Fred, Jr. *Harvard Poetic Renaissance: 1885–1910.* An unpublished Harvard dissertation, 1958.

Carman, Bliss and Hovey, Richard. *Songs from Vagabondia.* Boston: Small, Maynard and Company, 1907.

Cawein, Madison. *Poems.* New York: The Macmillan Company, 1911.

Chew, Samuel C. "Aestheticism and 'Decadence.' " In *A Literary History of England.* Edited by Albert C. Baugh. New York: Appleton-Century-Crofts, Inc., 1948, pp. 1475–84.

Cowley, Malcolm. *The Literary Situation.* New York: The Viking Press, 1954.

Ellmann, Richard. *Yeats: The Man and the Masks.* New York: The Macmillan Company, 1948.

Esslin, Martin. *The Theatre of the Absurd.* Garden City, New York: Doubleday & Company, Inc., 1961.

"Five New Volumes of Verse." *The New York Times,* April 28, 1906, p. 277.

Gangoly, O. C. *Landscape in Indian Literature and Art.* University of Lucknow, 1963.

Carin, Eugenio. *Italian Humanism.* Translated by Peter Munz. New York: Harper and Row, 1965.

Gohdes, Clarence. "New Voices in Verse." In *The Literature of the American People.* Edited by Arthur Hobson Quinn. New York: Appleton-Century-Crofts, Inc., 1951, pp. 721–36.

Gregory, Horace and Zaturenska, Marya. *A History of American Poetry, 1900–1940.* New York: Harcourt, Brace and Company, 1946.

Guiraud, Paul. "Allocution de M. Paul Guiraud." *Revue des Études Grecques* 18 (1905) : vi–xii.

Haldane, Seán. *The Fright of Time: Joseph Trumbull Stickney 1874–1904*. Ladysmith, Quebec: Ladysmith Press, 1970.

H[ale], S[winburne]. "Joseph Trumbull Stickney." *The Harvard Monthly* 39 (December, 1904) : 126–28.

Hapgood, Norman. *The Changing Years*. New York: Farrar & Rinehart, Inc., 1930.

Hauvette, Am. "Rapport de M. Am. Hauvette, Secrétaire, Sur Les Travaux et Les Concours de L'Année 1903–1904." *Revue des Études Grecques* 17 (1904) : xv–xxx.

Henry, David D. *William Vaughn Moody, A Study*. Boston: Bruce Humphries, Inc., 1934.

H[ubert], H[enri]. "J. Trumbull Stickney." *Revue Archéologique* 5, series 4 (January–June 1905) : 130–31.

H[ubert], H[enri]. "T. Stickney.—Les Sentences dans la poésie grecque d'Homère à Euripide." *L'Année Sociologique* 7 (1902–1903) : 670–73.

Kindilien, Carlin T. *American Poetry in the Eighteen Nineties*. Providence: Brown University Press, 1956.

Leslie, Shane. *American Wonderland*. London: Michael Joseph, Ltd., 1936.

———. *The Film of Memory*. London: Michael Joseph, Ltd., 1938.

Lodge, George Cabot. *Poems and Dramas*. 2 vols. Boston and New York: Houghton Mifflin Company, 1911.

———. Unpublished Letters in the Massachusetts Historical Society in Boston.

Lopez, Manuel D. "Joseph Trumbull Stickney (1874–1904)." *Bulletin of Bibliography and Magazine Notes* 26 (July–Sept. 1969) : 83–85.

Lovett, Robert Morss. *All Our Years*. New York: The Viking Press, 1948.

Lynch, William F., S. J. *Christ and Apollo, The Dimensions of the Literary Imagination*. New York: Sheed and Ward, Inc., 1960.

Martin, Jay. *Harvests of Change, American Literature 1865–1914*. Englewood Cliffs, New Jersey: Prentice-Hall, Inc., 1967.

Mason, Daniel Gregory. "At Harvard in the Nineties." *The New England Quarterly* 9 (March 1936) : 43–70.

————. *Music in My Time.* New York: The Macmillan Company, 1938.

Meyers, J. Wm. "A Complete Stickney Bibliography." *Twentieth Century Literature* 9 (January 1964) : 209–12.

————. "Stickney's Emancipation from Dogma." *Dasein Quarterly,* nos. 4 and 5 (Winter-Spring, 1965–1966) , pp. 175–85.

Moody, William Vaughn. *Letters to Harriet.* Edited by Percy MacKaye. Boston and New York: Houghton Mifflin Company, 1935.

————. *The Poems and Plays of William Vaughn Moody.* With an Introduction by John M. Manly. 2 vols. Boston and New York: Houghton Mifflin Company, 1912.

————. "The Poems of Trumbull Stickney." *The North American Review* 183 (November 16, 1906) : 1005–18.

————. *Some Letters of William Vaughn Moody.* Edited by Daniel Gregory Mason. Boston and New York: Houghton Mifflin Company, 1913.

Neff, Emery. *Edwin Arlington Robinson.* New York: William Sloane Associates, Inc., 1948.

Oppé, Adolf Paul. *Sandro Botticelli.* London and New York: Hodder and Stoughtoon, 1911.

Pascal, Blaise. *Pensées.* Translated by Martin Turnell. New York: Harper, 1962.

Payne, William Morton. Review of *Dramatic Verses. The Dial* 35 (July 16, 1903) : 39.

————. Review of *The Poems of Trumbull Stickney. The Dial* 40 (February 16, 1906) : 125.

Poulet, Georges. *Studies in Human Time.* Translated by Elliott Coleman. Baltimore: The Johns Hopkins Press, 1956.

Rahv, Philip, ed. *Discovery of Europe, The Story of American Experience in the Old World.* Boston: Houghton Mifflin Company, 1947.

Rand, E. K. "Joseph Trumbull Stickney." *The Harvard Graduates' Magazine* 13 (December 1904) : 242–44.

"Recent Poetry." *The Nation* 81 (December 21, 1905) : 506–8.

Reeves, James, and Seymour-Smith, Martin, eds. *A New Canon of English Poetry.* London: Heinemann Educational Books, Ltd., 1967.

Riggs, Thomas, Jr. "Prometheus 1900." *American Literature* 22 (January 1951) : 399–423.

———. "Trumbull Stickney (1874–1904)." *Dissertation Abstracts* 15 (1955) : 590.

———. *Trumbull Stickney (1874–1904).* Ann Arbor: University Microfilms, Inc., 1955. Publication No. 11,006.

Robinson, Edwin Arlington. *Collected Poems.* New York: The Macmillan Company, 1937.

———. *Selected Letters.* New York: The Macmillan Company, 1940.

Rodin, Auguste. *Art.* Translated from the French of Paul Gsell by Mrs. Romilly Fedden. Boston: Small, Maynard & Company, 1916.

Santayana, George. *The Letters of George Santayana.* Edited by Daniel Cory. New York: Charles Scribner's Sons, 1955.

———. *The Middle Span.* New York: Charles Scribner's Sons, 1945.

———. *My Host the World.* New York: Charles Scribner's Sons, 1953.

———. *The Poet's Testament.* New York: Charles Scribner's Sons, 1953.

Savage, Philip Henry. *The Poems of Philip Henry Savage.* Edited by Daniel Gregory Mason. Boston: Small, Maynard, and Company, 1901.

Stevenson, Elizabeth. *Henry Adams.* New York: The Macmillan Company, 1955.

Stickney, Joseph Trumbull. "The Beauvais Pottery." *The Nation* 75 (December 25, 1902) : 497.

———. *Bhagavad-Gītā.* Translated by Sylvain Lévi and J. T. Stickney. Paris, 1938. Reprinted Paris: A. Maisonneuve, 1964.

———. "Burckhardt (Jacob).—Griechische Kulturgeschichte." *L'Année Sociologique* 3 (1898–1899) : 310–14, 362–64; 5 (1900–1901) : 590–91.

————. "Captain Craig." *The Harvard Monthly* 37 (December 1903) : 99–102.

————. "Chocorua's Tenants." *The Harvard Monthly* 20 (May 1895) : 119–20.

————. *De Hermolai Barbari vita atque ingenio dissertationem.* Paris: *Lutetiae Parisiorum, Société Nouvelle de Librairie et d'Édition,* 1903.

————. "Dead-Levels." *The Harvard Monthly* 20 (April 1895) : 57–68.

————. *Dramatic Verses.* Boston: Charles E. Goodspeed, 1902.

————. "A Dull Study." *The Harvard Monthly* 19 (January 1895) : 162–68.

————. "The Great Refusal: Being Letters of a Dreamer in Gotham." *The Harvard Monthly* 20 (March 1895) : 38–40.

————. " 'Harvard Episodes'—Letter to the Editor." *The Harvard Monthly* 25 (February 1898) : 200–203.

————. "Herakleitos." *The Harvard Monthly* 19 (February 1895) : 175–80.

————. *Homage to Trumbull Stickney.* Poems selected and with an Introduction by James Reeves and Seán Haldane. London: Heinemann Educational Books, Ltd., 1968.

————. "Latin Poetry." *The Harvard Monthly* 21 (November 1895) : 88–90.

————. "Matters of Circumstance." *The Harvard Monthly* 18 (June 1894) : 147–67.

————. "Mr. Savage's Poems." *The Harvard Monthly* 20 (June 1895) : 155–58.

————. "Mr. William Watson." *The Harvard Monthly* 16 (June 1893) : 152–65.

————. "The Museum of St. Germain." *The Nation* 75 (November 20, 1902) : 398.

————. "Nature-Worship, Ancient and Modern." *The Harvard Monthly* 19 (November 1894) : 62–67.

————. "Odes and Other Poems." *The Harvard Monthly* 19 (January 1895) : 173–74.

————. "Plato and Platonism." *The Harvard Monthly* 18 (May 1894) : 134–36.

————. "Pliny and Letter-Writing." *The Harvard Monthly* 15 (January 1893) : 147–53.

————. *The Poems of Trumbull Stickney.* Edited by George Cabot Lodge, William Vaughn Moody, and John Ellerton Lodge. Boston and New York: Houghton Mifflin Company, 1905.

————. *The Poems of Trumbull Stickney.* Edited and with a biographical Introduction by Amberys R. Whittle. Foreword by Edmund Wilson. New York: Farrar, Straus & Giroux, Inc., 1972.

————. *Les Sentences dans la poésie grecque d'Homère à Euripide.* Paris: *Société Nouvelle de Librairie Et D'Édition, Librairie Georges Bellais,* 1903.

"Sunium." *Art and Archaeology* 5 (March 1917) : 171.

Taupin, René. *L'Influence du symbolisme français sur la poésie américaine.* Paris: Librairie Ancienne Honoré Champion, 1929.

Thorp, Willard. "Defenders of Ideality." In *Literary History of the United States: History.* 3rd ed. Edited by Robert E. Spiller *et al.* New York: The Macmillan Company, 1963, pp. 809–26.

Walker, Robert H. *The Poet and the Gilded Age, Social Themes in Late 19th Century Verse.* Philadelphia: University of Pennsylvania Press, 1963.

Weirick, Bruce. *From Whitman to Sandburg in American Poetry.* New York: The Macmillan Company, 1924.

Wilson, Edmund. " 'The Country I Remember.' " *The New Republic* 103 (October 14, 1940) : 529–30.

————. *Patriotic Gore.* New York: Oxford University Press, 1966.

Whittle, Amberys R. "The Dust of Seasons: Time in the Poetry of Trumbull Stickney." *The Sewanee Review* 74 (Autumn 1966) : 899–914.

Ziff, Larzer. *The American 1890s, Life and Times of a Lost Generation.* New York: The Viking Press, 1966.

Index

In this index, titles of poems are in italics, with *a, an,* or *the* placed at the end. First lines of untitled poems appear with quotation marks and are indexed with *a, an,* or *the* in their original order. Letter-by-letter alphabetizing is used in the index, but word-by-word order is used for Stickney's works listed under his name, as a convenience for those referring to my edition of *The Poems of Trumbull Stickney.*